STENCILING

Reyes Pujol-Xicoy
Juana Julià Casals

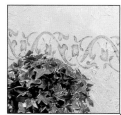

DT DECORATIVE TECHNIQUES

BARRON'S

STENCILING

Contents

chapter 3
PAINTING WITH STENCILS AND CHOOSING COLORS

METHODS OF STENCILING WITH A PAINTBRUSH

- Circular motion method, 36
- Stippling method, 37
- Painting with liquid paints, 38
- Painting with solid paints, 39
  Paints in sticks
  Paints in cream form
- Problems and solutions, 40
  Insufficient paint
  Your work is covered with dust
  The paint loses its consistency
  The edges of the stencil have become
    filled with paint
- Shading and volume with a brush, 42
  Shading with the same color
  Shading by layering colors

OTHER COLOR APPLICATORS

- Stenciling with a sponge roller, 44
- Stenciling with synthetic sponge or foam rubber, 45
- Stenciling with an aerosol, 46
  Shading with three-layered colors from
    dark to light
  Masks

COLOR

- How to choose the color, 48
- Cool and warm colors, 49
- Clean or aged colors, 49
- Mixtures of color, 50
  Primary colors
  Secondary colors
  Complementary colors
  Black and white

chapter 2
THE IMPORTANCE OF GOOD EQUIPMENT

MATERIALS FOR STENCILING

- Stencils, 20
  Stencils of manila oak tag or cardboard
  Polyester or acetate stencils
  Metal stencils
- Paintbrushes and other applicators, 22
  Paintbrushes
  Sponge applicators
  Aerosols
- Paint, 24
  Acrylic paints
  Oil paints
  Paints for fabrics
  Paints for ceramics and glass
  More about paint
- Other tools, 26

MATERIALS FOR PREPARING SURFACES

- Paints for priming surfaces, 28
- Materials for finishing and surface protection, 30
  Varnishes
  Waxes
  Aged finishes and patinas

CLEANING AND CONSERVING OF MATERIALS

- Cleaning and conserving stencils, 32
  How to clean stencils
  How to store stencils
- Cleaning applicators, 33

INTRODUCTION, 7

chapter 1
STENCILING: ORIGINS AND DEFINITION

WHAT STENCILING IS

- What it consists of, 10
- Characteristics, 10
- Where it can be applied, 11
- Why stenciling should be used, 12
  Its artistic function
  Its decorative function
  Its practical function
- Where to find it, 13

A TRIP THROUGH THE CENTURIES

- The Orient, 14
- Europe, 15
  Italy
  France
  England
- America, 17
- Stenciling today, 17

chapter 4
DESIGNING AND MAKING THE STENCILS

THE DESIGN OF THE STENCILS

- Materials for making stencils, 54
  Tools for drawing stencils
  Tools for cutting out stencils
- Choosing the design, 56
  Sources of inspiration
  Elaborating on an existing design
  Choosing something new
- What a stencil is like, 58
  Windows
  Bridges
  Simple and multiple stencils
  Registration marks
- Composing a design for stenciling, 61
  Enclosed compositions in sequence
  Open compositions in sequence
  Isolated motifs that can be freely combined
  Enclosed combined motifs

TECHNIQUES FOR DESIGNING AND CUTTING OUT A STENCIL

- Isolating and simplifying the design, 62
- Dividing the drawing into several stencils, 63
- Cutting out a stencil, 64
  Using a craft knife
  Using an electric cutter
  With scissors
- How to correct mistakes, 66
- Designing a printed pattern, 67

TRICKS OF THE TRADE

- Proximity of colors, 68
- Layering the shapes, 68
  A flower
  Checkered fabric
  Cord
  Clouds and trees
  Grapes
  An apple can be a pear
- Economizing on stencils, 70
  A Grecian urn with leaves and fruit
- Stenciling over the edges, 70
  A frieze of leaves
  Waves
- Combining two designs by using two stencils, 71

chapter 5
STENCILING ON DIFFERENT SURFACES

STENCILING ON WALLS

- Preparing the walls, 75
  Cracked walls
  Smooth walls
  Textured walls
  Papered walls
- Base colors, 77
- Friezes, 78
  Horizontal friezes
  Stenciling a frieze with spaces in the design
  Stenciling friezes with continuous designs
  How to stencil corners
  Vertical friezes
  Framing doors and windows with friezes
  Doing panels
  Combining individual motifs
  Centralized individual motifs
  Off-center individual motifs
  A composition with individual motifs
- Prints, 88
- Tricks of the trade, 90
- Correcting mistakes, 91
- Adding the look of aging, 91

STENCILING ON WOOD

- Preparing the surface, 93
  Raw or clean wood
  Painted wood in poor condition
  Painted wood in good condition
- Stenciling on raw or clean wood, 95
- Stenciling on plastic paint, 95
- Stenciling on varnish or gloss paint, 96
- Imitation wood inlay, 97
- How to protect your work with varnish, 98
  Varnishing
  Patinas to age the wood finish
  Crackling
  Waxing

STENCILING ON TEXTILES

- The types of fabric that can be stenciled, 100
- How to stencil on fabric, 102
  The importance of the base color
- Stenciled household linens, 106
  Imitation cross-stitch
  Imitation appliqué
  Imitation embroidery
- Stenciling patchwork, 108

- Stenciling on upholstery, 110
  Stenciling a footstool

STENCILING ON OTHER SURFACES

- Stenciling onto lamp shades, 113
- Stenciling on vegetable fibers and cotton, 114
- Stenciling on paper, 115
  Some tips on stenciling on paper
  Stenciled stationery
- Stenciling on ceramics, 116
  Cold ceramic stenciling
  Stenciling on terra-cotta
  Warm ceramic stenciling
- Stenciling on glass, 118
  Imitation etching
  Colored stenciling
- Stenciling on metal objects, 120
  Preparing the surface
  Stenciling on zinc
  Stenciling on brass

chapter 6
ADVANCED TECHNIQUES

BRIDGELESS STENCILING

- Origin, 124
- Characteristics of bridgeless stenciling, 125
- Sources of inspiration, 125
- How to do theorem stenciling, 126
  Preparing the design
  Drawing the stencils
  Cutting out the stencils
  Marking the stencils
  Preparing the palette
- Theorem stenciling a basket of fruit, 129
  Defining planes

STENCILING TROMPE L'OEIL

- What trompe l'oeil is, 132
- Trompe l'oeil and theorem stenciling, 133
- Procedure for painting a trompe l'oeil, 134
  The base drawing
  Composition of the elements
  How to transfer the design onto the wall
- Stenciling a trompe l'oeil, 136

GLOSSARY, 142

Introduction

In the huge field of techniques for decorative painting, stenciling is perhaps the most ancient, the most popular, the easiest to carry out, and the most versatile. Stenciling is one of the most attractive and pleasing methods of decorating any surface by hand, as it allows you to choose from a wide range of designs and styles.

This book is aimed at those who take pleasure in creating warm surroundings and enjoy decorating with an artistic personal touch. The material presented is geared to represent graphically, clearly, and simply the step-by-step development of the many varieties of stenciling techniques. These techniques range from the most traditional use of stencil, the frieze, to the most inventive, such as imitating wood inlay, patchwork, reproducing etched glass, or stenciling optical illusions.

After the first two chapters on the origin of stenciling, its functions, and necessary tools and materials, this book focuses on basic techniques, with special emphasis on stencil design and painting methods. The last two chapters describe methods for decorating a variety of surfaces with stencils, how each one should be prepared, and the way to tackle a project in order to achieve a satisfactory result. All this is done by presenting original projects, ideas, and tricks of the trade, beautifully photographed to inspire the reader's creativity. The book concludes with the advanced techniques of theorem (or bridgeless) stenciling and the creation of optical illusions (or trompe l'oeil), two innovative uses of the medium that are not widely known.

Stenciling:
origins and definition

Stenciling is one of the simplest, most economical, effective, and creative ways of decorating a surface. It can be adapted to all kinds of decorative styles and one does not require a great deal of artistic training in order to achieve original and attractive results. Its versatility, diversity, and great elegance are the key to its use by all civilizations down through the centuries for adorning dwellings, churches, palaces, fabrics, garments, pottery, and tiles. It can add beauty and warmth to any surface, rejuvenate old and scarred walls or floors, and can be adapted to all the shapes and styles of any room.

What stenciling is

Stenciling is a method, a tool, and a medium. It is the perfect alternative to wallpaper and freehand decorating. Stenciling is the method of choice for anyone who wants to design and decorate by hand in an original way that is expressive of unique ideas and personal style.

What it consists of

The term *stencil* has its origins in the Middle Ages and comes from the Latin word *scintilla* and from the French *étinceller*, which mean to spangle or to brighten with stars. In English, the word *stenciling* comes, of course, from the object, the *stencil*, used to outline an area to be painted.

From the point of view of technique, stenciling consists of applying paint or pigment over shapes cut out from a piece of impermeable paper that is placed over the surface to be decorated. It is this cut-out paper that is called a stencil. Stencils can be used over and over again until they finally deteriorate. The great advantage of stenciling over freehand painting is that a single cut-out design can be repeated over the length of any space as many times as necessary without having to be drawn and redrawn.

Tablecloth and set of 12 napkins in cotton stenciled with a grapevine, bunches of grapes, and butterflies. Stenciling is much quicker than embroidering. This tablecloth was finished in a week and has 50 butterflies, all stenciled in different colors.

Characteristics

One thing that is characteristic about stenciling is its smooth and even finish. The design appears to emerge from the surface that has been painted. Other important characteristics are the shapes, which are partitioned and separated by a space known as a "bridge"—these serve as the design and structure of the stencil—and the possibility of repeating the design as many times as necessary with the same stencil.

Where it can be applied

There is an enormous range of application for stenciling, and it knows no frontiers, as it can be adapted perfectly to all surfaces. Ideal for stenciling is the wide range of varieties and sizes of old or functional furniture, inside and outside walls, wood and terra-cotta floors, cloth, floor mats, glassware, mirrors, and so on. It is simply a question of using the right tools and paints for each.

Because of its versatility, stenciling awakens our creativity by urging us to modify and personalize our environment. It provides unique solutions to our physical and emotional needs, and the final result is the creation of very particular and nontransferable universes.

These doors to a dressing room were stenciled with a classical motif, laurel wreaths, on an antiqued background. In spite of the simplicity of the design, the doors show great elegance.

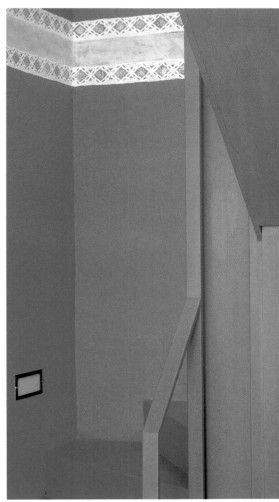

Over the indigo blue walls of a dry goods store, a white frieze, with stenciling that is reminiscent of Swiss embroidery, is striking.

Stenciling is more and more frequently used for decorating children's rooms. In this example, the wood panel was decorated with a tale about rabbits, depicting a simple, engaging childhood theme.

Stenciling on unusual surfaces, such as this fiber mat, can be very attractive. Very original effects, like this imitation zebra skin, can be obtained. Designs can be stenciled to carry through patterns in curtains and furniture.

Why stenciling should be used

Stenciling is not only a perfect decorative complement to furniture, paint, and fabric, but it can also be a useful tool for solving practical problems such as the repetition of a design to save time, or for correcting structural defects to save expense. Stenciling is an effective camouflage for imperfections in the surface of plaster or paint.

Its artistic function

Practicality is not at odds with creativity. Contemporary artists and graphic designers use stenciling to repeat shapes in their paintings or in their commercial artwork.

Thus stenciling becomes a practical tool to enhance and to make more efficient any artistic project, from a sophisticated and complex painting all the way down to cake decoration.

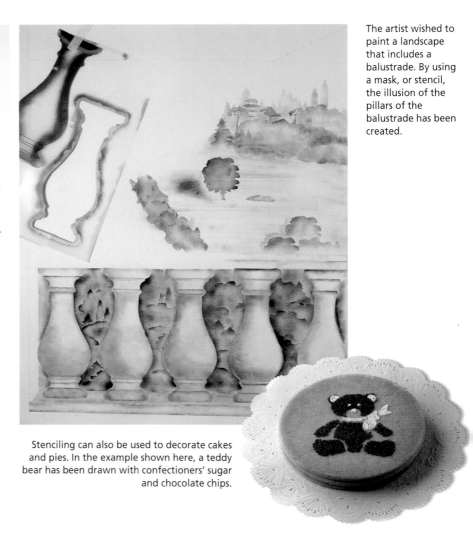

The artist wished to paint a landscape that includes a balustrade. By using a mask, or stencil, the illusion of the pillars of the balustrade has been created.

Stenciling can also be used to decorate cakes and pies. In the example shown here, a teddy bear has been drawn with confectioners' sugar and chocolate chips.

Its decorative function

Stenciling brightens up corners, walls, and furniture, and gives them an original touch. It lends a finishing touch to blank spaces and cuts costs. A frieze can create a greater sense of order and harmony in a wall, a corner, or on a floor, tying them into the room's decor. An outdated piece of furniture can be transformed into a new decorative element simply and inexpensively. The pattern of curtains can be repeated on walls, creating beautiful and unique visual harmonies. A well-thought-out decoration, stenciled onto a wall, will put space to good use while avoiding unnecessary clutter.

In this space, stenciling had a double purpose. On the one hand, the architectural frieze, the Greek key, makes up for the lack of a molding where the wall meets the ceiling. On the other hand, because the wall is curved, a painted scene would have appeared distorted, so the peacocks, used here as a motif, fulfill their decorative function perfectly.

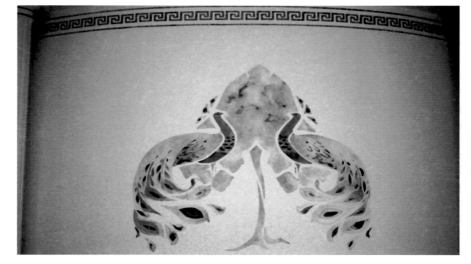

Its practical function

In most homes, structural elements are found that distort or mar the harmony of an area of space. Stenciling makes practical sense when it:

• **Corrects defects**
A narrow corridor can be widened optically by dividing the wall horizontally in two using a frieze, a continuous horizontal design. A ceiling that is too high can be made to appear lower by painting a frieze at a height of about 8 feet (2.5 m). A door can be disguised with an optical illusion.

• **Enhances strong points**
A pillar decorated with climbing ivy can become the center of attraction of a room.

• **Imitates architectural elements**
The joining of ceiling and wall can be embellished with a frieze stenciled around the perimeter of a room.

• **Imitates embroidery**
A tablecloth stenciled with the same design as the dinner service or a cushion with initials is easy to do.

This corridor is long and narrow. One way to widen it and give it some warmth is to combine a warm background color with a stenciled frieze at 40 inches (102 cm) from the floor.

The walls of this bedroom are covered with navy blue silk. To finish off the top of the walls, instead of using a molding, a frieze of large flowers provided a much more original solution.

Where to find it

Though they may be hard to recognize, we are surrounded by shapes produced by means of stencils. They can take the form of traffic signs in garages and on roads, on pedestrian crossings, and bike paths. Packages are lettered with them.

Beyond its ordinary and industrial uses, stenciling is commonly found in historical places such as churches and palaces, in grand villas, and in Art Nouveau or Victorian houses, where its magnificent decoration adorns ceilings and walls.

More and more frequently, cities designate specific areas for cycling enthusiasts. A perfectly recognizable symbol for a person from any part of the world is a bicycle painted with the help of a stencil.

This photo was taken in Barcelona, Spain, but it could be of any city in the world. Urban language is universal. Just by using stencils, the same signs can be reproduced anywhere.

A trip through the centuries

It is not known exactly when and where the technique of painting over a mask, later to be known as stenciling, originated. There are no documents to bear witness, although it is most probable that several different civilizations practiced stenciling, using different techniques. The history of stenciling has been reconstructed from the few fragments that have survived until the present time.

A marvelous ancient Japanese stencil with the shapes made out of wood and held down with mesh. Note the filigree work on the shapes that make up the design.

This ancient stencil is of Japanese origin. The shapes were made with very thin wood, the entire design held down by a mesh of silk threads, framed by the wood itself. The close-up reveals the precision with which the sheet of wood was cut.

The Orient

Although it cannot be confirmed exactly, it seems to be generally accepted that in China, about 3000 B.C., masks perforated with needles were being used to paint on silk. The first evidence of the existence of stenciling, however, dates from the first century A.D. This evidence comes by way of Sir Aurel Stein's discovery in 1907 of the famous Caves of the Hundred Buddhas in Tunhuang, China. Painted silks were found there with images of Buddha outlined with stencils. Also found were the original designs, made using a kind of tough, leathery paper. These designs were outlined with very fine holes. In order to transfer the design onto the cloth, the stencil was hammered with chalk that was forced through the holes, then the lines were traced and the drawing was colored in freehand.

Although, strictly speaking, this technique cannot be called stenciling, it is an important forerunner of its later development. Subsequently, a method was invented that consisted of using a special ink that acted like an acid and ate through the paper, thus achieving perfectly silhouetted designs. From China by way of the commercial silk roads that were established with neighboring countries, the technique of stenciling reached other Oriental civilizations. It was widely used in

Japan, for example, and it was there that the technique reached a high degree of refinement.

The first evidence of Japanese stenciling dates from 600 A.D. Still a popular art form in Japan, the stencil is known as *katagami,* and the technique of stenciling with dyes is known as *katazome,* used for dying silk with designs inspired by nature. In ancient times, stencils were crafted of mulberry wood, then pressed and waterproofed in such a way as to obtain fine, durable sheets that, at the same time, permitted precise and detailed cutting. This was done with a sharp knife, crafting two stencils that were glued together with adhesive resin. The result was a very durable, precisely carved stenciling tool. Alongside this technique, the stencils perforated with fine holes were also used.

In the course of time, stenciling reached Siam (Thailand), Persia (Iran), and India. In each of these countries, the subject matter was quite different, although the method adopted was similar to the Chinese method: chalk applied through small holes. In Siam, nature-inspired subjects predominated, while in Persia, stenciling was limited to the representation of sacred writing. In India, artists stretched the limits of geometrical drawings in search of ideal spatial designs consistent with Indian philosophy, whic is concerned with the search for perfection in all things.

This Japanese stencil is made from stiff cardboardlike paper. In the close-up you can see the holes made along the outlines of its very beautiful design; the powdered pigment, held in a fabric bag, is pounded through these holes.

Europe

The commercial routes from the Orient brought stenciling to Europe at around the same time as it reached other Eastern countries. It first arrived in Italy, then, in the early Middle Ages, the technique reached France and England.

Medieval craftsmen combined free-hand painting with the use of stencils to create a wide variety of ornamental motifs.

The evolution of stenciling was irregular in the centuries that followed until it came into broad and frequent use at the end of the seventeenth century. Then, and until the nineteenth century, with the birth of Art Nouveau in the first decades of the twentieth century, it reached its greatest splendor.

Italy

In Italy, children were taught to write using stencils during the time of the Roman Empire. Political giants like the emperor Justinian and, later, Charlemagne signed their documents with stenciled initials. The artists who painted frescoes from the Middle Ages through the Renaissance used masks perforated with needles to transfer sketches onto their walls.

France

French art history is rich with stenciling. In the Middle Ages, stenciling was used for decorating playing cards, for designing the glorious wallpapers France is known for, for printing fabrics, and for illustrating books. French book illustrators were craftsmen who used stencils to color the silhouettes they printed using woodcuts. This twofold combination—stenciling and woodcuts—spread throughout Europe.

Although it has been said that it was in the decoration of playing cards that stenciling was most often used, it must not be forgotten that France was the great driving force behind wallpaper design, and that the city of Rouen was the center of its manufacture. Jean Papillon (circa 1688), considered to be the father of wallpaper, was one of those who developed stenciling for coloring woodcut prints on paper. From the end of the fifteenth century until the middle of the nineteenth, stenciled paper was used in numerous religious paintings to imitate drapery; it was used to decorate houses, and even to illustrate newspapers.

England

However, England was the country in which stenciling had an extraordinary boom. It is known that in the thirteenth century, Henry III loved to have his walls painted in green and adorned with stenciled golden stars. At that time, and for almost a century afterward, stenciling was used in churches for painting emblems, draperies and fleurs de lis, monograms, suns, and floral patterns. In the sixteenth century, during Tudor times, the stenciling of geometric patterns became popular in the houses of the gentry. Stenciling also became popular among those who were less wealthy, who used it to decorate flocked paper and thus imitate the rich velvet tapestries that hung in the houses of aristocrats. Also at this time, paper stamped with woodcuts and colored with stencils became fashionable. Instead of using pigments to color in the shapes, powdered wool was used, which was applied through the stencil onto a glue-covered surface. But there is evidence that stenciling was not held in high regard by some. The Company of Painters and Dyers of London, in literature of the time, denounced the practice of stenciling, stating, "It is false and deceitful work, besides being damaging to the art of painting, an obstacle to genius and a spur to laziness and sloth for all apprentices to the art."

The eighteenth century was one of the golden ages of stenciling. This can be directly attributed, first, to an Act of Parliament in 1702, imposing heavy taxes on "painted, printed or dyed" paper, which made wallpaper prohibitively expensive. Stenciling then became the ideal and most economical alternative for decorating walls. Second, the belief became widespread that carpets were unhealthy, as they accumulated dirt and were hard to clean; therefore, the application of stencils to painted wood floors was developed. The taxes on wallpaper were abolished in the nineteenth century and, once again, its use flourished. Though stenciling lost popularity, its use was continued for church decoration. It was this genre that was largely responsible for its survival.

William Morris, a leading figure in the great Arts and Crafts movement in Europe, was responsible for the rebirth of stenciling during the Victorian Age in the nineteenth century. England was at the vanguard of the Industrial Revolution, and played a leading role in the large-scale production of fabric, furniture, and decorative goods. Morris's philosophy was responsible for the revival of traditional crafts, bringing them into the category of art. He was concerned with elevating the ordinary lives of people through their surroundings and artifacts. He feared the devaluation that the rise of machinery would cause. He promoted furniture, fabric, and interior designs related to the idea of more beautiful, comfortable, and pleasant dwellings where utility and beauty went hand in hand, restoring the dignity of the individual through art.

Morris's ideas spread and flourished, picked up by decorators and architects of the time. It was during this time that William Burgues developed the use of Gothic designs for walls, ceilings, and furniture. Morris's influence stoked the imaginations of such great Art Nouveau decorators and architects as Charles Rennie Mackintosh, and persisted until the years before World War I.

Victorian designs are still being used today as decorative motifs for stenciling on walls, fabric, wallpaper, glass objects, tiles, and an array of other surfaces.

Detail of the mural, done in 1924, that decorates the ceiling of the Royal Palace at Pedralbes in Barcelona, Spain. Stenciling was used to reproduce the decorative motifs that are repeated on the walls of the chamber.

Art Nouveau was influenced by William Morris's philosophy. This original frieze belongs to a Spanish house decorated in the modernist style.

America

During the sixteenth and seventeenth centuries, the Europeans who emigrated to America introduced stenciling to the new continent. It is thanks to traveling artists from New England that this medium reached the height of its popularity from the mid-1700s to the end of the nineteenth century. During that time, it became the fashion for wealthier families on America's east coast to decorate the walls of their houses with murals done on wallpaper imported from Europe, depicting Greek gardens or palace halls. Owing to the high cost of such decoration, artists were brought over who adapted the European style to local surroundings, thus creating an original manner of expression that was taken up by the colonists to give a touch of refinement to even the most humble homes. This brought about an enormous increase in the popularity of stenciling. Most of its subject matter was concerned with everyday surroundings: leaves, flowers, fruit, bells, birds, stars, and pinecones, which were a symbol of colonial hospitality. These designs were repeated on furniture, walls, floors, crockery, chimneys, and bedspreads. Stenciled floor coverings were particularly fashionable, their designs imitating beautiful, but expensive, handwoven rugs. These floor coverings were as practical and portable as rugs, but could be easily changed around and transported into another house.

For reasons of economy and practicality, stenciling was used for painting on velvet wall hangings. This was done using a technique known as *theorem stenciling,* which consists of painting through stencils cut out according to a numerical division of the design, with the aim of closely imitating reality. The majority of designs used in the United States were the work of itinerant artists of the time.

Stenciling was used in prehistoric cave painting, as can be seen in these paintings stenciled on the walls of the "Cave of Hands," south of Perito Moreno in Argentina. The negative impressions of the human hands were done by laying the hand against the wall and coloring around it, in other words, by using the hand as a stencil.

During the nineteenth century, although mass-produced goods began to replace handwork, a generation of proficient craftworkers began producing furniture and other objects decorated with stenciling to be sold in their own stores.

Stenciling today

Today, the revival of tastes for old-style decorations allows us to integrate elements from the past into modern homes. Stenciling is one of these elements. This revival can be attributed to a variety of factors, but largely to the research done by craftspeople and designers who are fascinated by the possibilities of this technique, and to the publication of old Victorian and American designs. Two such researchers are Adele Bishop and Lynn Le Grice, to whom we owe the recovery and the popularization of many old designs, as well as the creation and commercialization of new ones, and the production of stenciling products for the general public.

These days, stenciling not only interests decorators, antique collectors, and craftworkers, but also attracts those with a creative interest who appreciate the originality, versatility, and warmth of personalized, handcrafted decoration such as stenciling. This art form has found its own place in modern times and fills the gap that cannot be filled by commercially produced designs and products.

Stenciling technique and imagery can be endlessly creative, adapting to any style and surface. And while it is true that wallpaper and decorative friezes can be found on the market in a variety of patterns, stenciling provides a unique quality quite different from wallpaper, allowing us to repeat the design on other surfaces as well. Apart from its being an alternative to wallpaper, this technique is quicker and easier to apply than freehand painting.

The importance of good equipment

The recent boom in stenciling as a decorative art has resulted in the appearance of an enormous variety of materials on the market. This sudden interest in the use of arts and crafts in decorating has reached such a level of popularity that it inevitably encourages manufacturers to improve quality and designs as well as to make materials affordable for the general public. Having the right equipment and paints is as important to the production of quality results as is the beauty of the designs and colors used. The use of the right equipment will also greatly simplify the task. This chapter covers a wide variety of indispensable materials and accessories for carrying out any project, however complex it may be.

Materials for stenciling

Although the range of materials for stenciling is very wide, not all of it is necessary for every result. It is important, however, to understand the potential of each in order to choose the most suitable ones. The most indispensable things are: stencils and materials for making them, paintbrushes, and paints.

Stencils

Most stencils are made from impermeable paper or other materials that do not break down when paint is applied, and also are not damaged when they are cleaned. Cardboard and thin sheets of metal are also excellent.

In art supply or craft stores, ready-designed stencils can be found for use by beginners. These are of simple design, perfectly adaptable to any decorative style and all kinds of spaces. They come in a variety of materials.

Designs are available for all types of surroundings and needs. Their prices vary depending on the material used and the complexity of the design.

A selection of stencils made from different materials: (from left to right) stencil of a fruit motif made with manila oak tag, a small metal flower stencil, and a variety of stencils made of waterproof polyester paper and thick plastic.

Stencils of manila oak tag or cardboard

The first of these can be obtained in art or craft stores. It is opaque and ocher in color. It has a variety of uses but its disadvantage is that it cannot be washed. Thick cardboard can be used. Water- or greaseproof paper may be hard to find but can be easily made (see picture at right). Such waterproof cardboard is very practical for working with large monochrome designs and for painting with aerosol spray paint.

Manila paper is a very old name given to this type of paper. If you cannot find it in a store, you can buy cardboard and waterproof it with linseed oil thinned with a little turpentine.

Polyester or acetate stencils

These are made from polyester paper (translucent) or acetate (transparent) and can be found ready-cut in a variety of sizes. If you intend to prepare your own stencils, polyester paper and acetates come in different thicknesses. It is preferable to choose a medium thickness, as it is easier to cut and will not break down with washing. This is a practical material for repeated designs in several colors, first because its transparency allows for alignment with the rest of your design, while its flexibility makes it adaptable to awkward places such as corners and rounded edges. Second, it can be washed repeatedly without deteriorating.

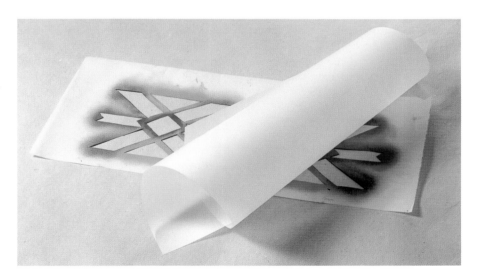

Polyester paper is translucent and flexible. It is easy to find in stores that sell materials for technical drawing. It is probably the most useful and popular product for stenciling.

Metal stencils

These stencils last a lifetime. They are sold already cut out and the designs are usually small. Their substantial thickness sometimes makes it difficult to outline shapes precisely. Also, they lack flexibility, and therefore cannot be adapted to angular or round surfaces.

Metal stencils are the most durable and also the most difficult to find. Antique stencils can often be found at antique stores and fairs; these were sometimes used to mark fabrics with the manufacturer's name.

Paintbrushes and other applicators

In the past, all kinds of materials were used for applying paint through the cut-outs in a stencil. These ranged from linen bags (called pounce bags) to wool or cotton wrapped around a stick, sea sponges, brushes, and even pieces of potato. Today, paintbrushes, sponge applicators, and aerosols are commonly used and readily available in the marketplace.

Pounce bags, small bags of fine cotton material perforated with pinholes, held powdered pigment and were used for paint application.

Applying paint by saturating a toothbrush with pigment and flicking the bristles with the finger is a method commonly used now, even with younger children, functioning much like an airbrush.

Paintbrushes

The best-known and most frequently used utensils for stenciling are paintbrushes especially designed for this purpose. The classic stenciling brush is rounded, of short, dense white hogshair, its bristles cut bluntly to the same length. It is designed so that the paint does not bleed underneath the edges of the stencil. A brush's quality depends on the bristle used to make it, the bristle's density, and its smoothness.

Top-quality hogshair retains and distributes the paint with the greatest of precision. The design of the hogshair stencil brush makes it suitable for all types of finishes: transparent and smooth, if used in a circular motion, or deeper and denser if the color is stippled on (see page 37). It is useful to have brushes of several different types and sizes on hand when working. The stiffer ones can be used for priming backgrounds, and the softer ones for shading and transparency. Thick brushes are used for large designs and finer ones for small drawings.

Stenciling brushes come in many sizes and differ in quality. It is not necessary to start with a large collection as, with practice, experience, and exploration, you will find the brushes that work best for you. Here are some points to keep in mind:

Even beginners should use brushes of good **quality.** The bristles should be soft and flexible, with the capacity to create subtle and transparent results. When properly cared for, brushes will last for many years.

Regarding **size,** as a general rule, it is best to use a thick brush for painting backgrounds and large shapes, a medium-sized brush for medium-sized shapes, and a small one for the smallest shapes.

As far as **number** is concerned, you will need one for each color, but when starting out, three or four should be enough.

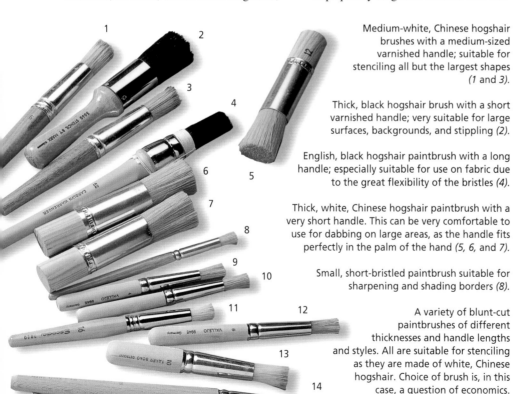

Medium-white, Chinese hogshair brushes with a medium-sized varnished handle; suitable for stenciling all but the largest shapes (1 and 3).

Thick, black hogshair brush with a short varnished handle; very suitable for large surfaces, backgrounds, and stippling (2).

English, black hogshair paintbrush with a long handle; especially suitable for use on fabric due to the great flexibility of the bristles (4).

Thick, white, Chinese hogshair paintbrush with a very short handle. This can be very comfortable to use for dabbing on large areas, as the handle fits perfectly in the palm of the hand (5, 6, and 7).

Small, short-bristled paintbrush suitable for sharpening and shading borders (8).

A variety of blunt-cut paintbrushes of different thicknesses and handle lengths and styles. All are suitable for stenciling as they are made of white, Chinese hogshair. Choice of brush is, in this case, a question of economics. Paintbrushes with varnished handles are more expensive than those of unvarnished wood. These tend to stand up better to constant use and washing (9 to 15).

Sponge applicators

Foam rubber rollers and applicators are made from very compact synthetic sponge and allow you to paint smoothly, though without obtaining many subtleties. They are useful for preliminary studies, for priming the background for large areas, and then for finishing the work with brushes.

Several types of sponge roller are available, in different densities, with different types of fixed or interchangeable handles.

Sponge applicators fixed to a handle are manufactured for wall and trim painting and can be used for stenciling as well. A piece of fine synthetic sponge or upholstery foam can also be used.

Examples of stenciling with different applicators

Stenciling with a paintbrush and using a circular motion.

This stencil was also done with a paintbrush, but by stippling.

Here, a piece of upholstery foam has been used to apply the paint. Depending on the pressure exerted, and the density of the foam, the mark appears more or less stippled.

In this stencil, painted with an aerosol, the edges are blurred and the color is fine, even, and more intense than with other applicators.

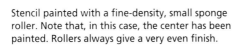

Stencil painted with a fine-density, small sponge roller. Note that, in this case, the center has been painted. Rollers always give a very even finish.

Aerosols

Spray paints can be plastic based or synthetic enamel. This last type includes paint sold for use on automobiles. Applying it can be complicated, as it requires a certain amount of experience and the diffuser nozzle tends to get clogged. Holding the can upside down and depressing the nozzle will clear it. After a few trial runs, you can use it on any surface, obtaining some very interesting results. Its characteristic property is that it is fast-drying

Automobile aerosols, easy to obtain, can be a good choice for practicing technique. When working with these, it is essential to use a face mask, as the fine spray is toxic.

Paint

The first step when beginning a stenciling project is choosing the paint. There is a large range of qualities of paints available. Paints suitable for stenciling include, apart from acrylics and oils, a wide variety of special paints for fabrics, glass, tiles, and so on. Paints can be water based or oil based, and each has a different solvent. Some are more watery; others are thicker. A beginner should use the latter as they are easier to handle. Trials with a few samples will help you to find the most suitable paint for achieving the effects you prefer while demonstrating the medium's capacity.

Acrylic paints

These are water-based paints that can be thinned with water. Brushes are also cleaned with water before the paint dries, after which time the pigment is waterproof and permanent. They come in three different versions: jars of liquid, tubes, and jars of acrylic with a creamy texture that may be thinned, all suitable for beginners. Acrylic dries quickly and covers well. Its pigment is strong and true. The painted surface dries perfectly even and opaque with a matte finish. Acrylics adhere perfectly to the majority of surfaces and they do not fade. They can be applied to interior or exterior walls, clean wood, paper, fiber mats, clay, plaster, and most other surfaces.

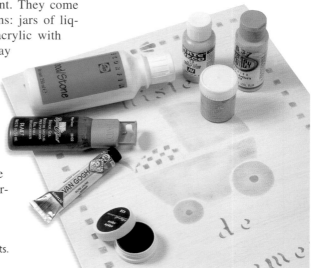

Acrylic paints.

Oil paints

These come in tubes or oil sticks. They are paints with a vegetable oil base, such as linseed or poppy, and are dissolved with turpentine or paint thinner. Because they are very slow-drying, you have to take great care when using several stencils on top of one another, as successive layers of paint may smudge. The stick forms are most practical for beginners as sticks are more easily handled and dry faster. Once dry, oil paints are very resistant to damage and retain the brightness of their tones. Their color, transparency, and adherence to surfaces (and consequently their durability) make them a perfect medium for high-quality work. They are ideal for painting on all kinds of varnished or lacquered surfaces, indoors or outdoors. They are not practical for use on fabrics.

Oil paints.

Paints for fabrics

Fabric paint is also water based. It differs from acrylics in that it is smoother and more transparent and keeps its flexibility when dry. In most cases, once the paint is completely dry, heat has to be applied for a few minutes in order to permanently fix the color. It then remains unaltered when washed. These paints are suitable for cotton, linen, or mixed fibers. Because there are a great variety of manufacturers of fabric paints, it is a good idea to experiment with several to explore their capacity and durability.

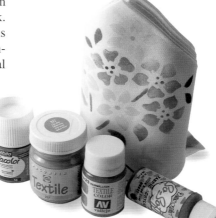

Paints for fabrics.

Paints for ceramics and glass

These come as water or oil based, and either can be used for both glass and ceramic surfaces. Their chief characteristic is their capacity to adhere to glazed, nonporous surfaces. Paints for cold application to ceramic surfaces, as opposed to firing glazes, have appeared relatively recently. These are also usable on other shiny, nonporous materials such as acrylic plastic, glazed porcelain, plastics, and tiles. Paints for glass are more transparent.

Paints for ceramics.

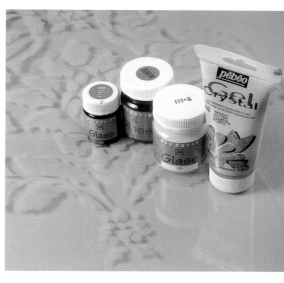

Paints for glass.

More about paint

In addition to all of the above, there are other factors that are useful to know and keep in mind about the application of paint for stenciling in general.

• Oil and water don't mix
An oil- or water-based paint must be used to prepare or prime the surface for stenciling. Here one must take care to choose a primer that will accept the applied paint and hold it permanently.

Basically, water-based paints are used on a naked surface or water-receptive primer, whereas oil-based paints may be used on an oil- or acrylic-based background. However, water-based paints cannot be used on an oil-based background or primer, as they will not adhere permanently.

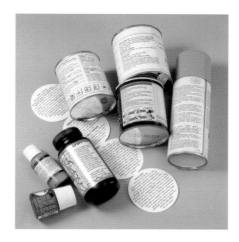

• Read the instructions
When selecting your paints, you will most often find all the information you will need in the manufacturer's instructions regarding method of application, type of solvent, drying time, and so on.

Most paint products for stenciling contain precise information from the manufacturer concerning the product's specific properties. Although this book describes general characteristics, new products are constantly appearing on the market. When in doubt, always consult the manufacturer's instructions.

• A specific paint for each material
Paint needs a porous surface in order to adhere to the support. There are shiny surfaces with particularly nonabsorbent properties that require a special type of paint for stenciling. For best results, bear in mind the characteristics of different types of paint as discussed on these two pages.

This tile has been decorated with a paint that is unsuitable for a glazed surface. Once it is dry, the paint can be rubbed or rinsed off.

Blue, water-based plastic paint has been used on a background prepared with an oil-based synthetic enamel paint. The paint slides over the surface and won't adhere.

Other tools

A good set of equipment consists of a wide variety of materials, some of which may seem unrelated to actual stenciling but which can be pressed into service in creative ways in order to accomplish a particular task or produce a unique effect. It is a good idea to have a rich assortment of such tools and materials from which to select for each particular project. This will greatly facilitate your work and keep you in better spirits.

A great variety of materials and accessories will be discussed here, putting special emphasis on those that, from a practical point of view, make the job easier and less demanding. Our idea is that this wide range of suggestions may help the stencil artist choose those materials most suited to each project.

A wooden or metal level should be used for lining up a frieze along the length of a wall, keeping a straight line in relation to floor and ceiling.

Drying retardants are essential for maintaining the consistency of the paint for the length of the work process, especially when tackling such big jobs as stenciling walls.

Tape measures can be flexible, such as those used for dressmaking, or rigid. Rigid measures are more convenient for measuring large surfaces as they may extend to 3 or 4 feet (91–122 cm) or longer. For small objects or furniture, dressmakers' tape measures are perfectly adequate and often preferable.

A painters' or carpenters' ladder will, of course, be needed for high places. If you need to work across a wide space, the ladder should be lightweight and well anchored so that you can relax and paint unimpeded.

If you prefer, you may want to protect your hands, especially when painting with aerosol or oil paints. Surgical gloves are useful for this purpose as they are thin and do not reduce sensitivity in your hands. They should fit well and not be too tight or too loose, again so that you are unimpeded as you work.

Stencils have to be fixed to the surfaces that are going to be painted, or the paint may run underneath. A very effective tool for this purpose is a spray mount. Painters' adhesive tape is another option. When using aerosols, in order to prevent the nozzle from getting blocked, hold the can upside down when you have finished and depress the nozzle until it finishes spraying.

It is easier if you use small amounts of paint at a time for your stenciling, rather than using it straight from the can, as it is apt to dry out before you have used up the contents. Any container will do, from commercial palettes to recycled aluminum or plastic trays.

Paper towels and absorbent rags are important to have on hand for drying your paintbrush as well as unloading excess paint before painting. These should be changed as they become saturated.

For portability and to keep your materials well organized, a tackle box or easily washable canvas bag, with lots of pockets, can be used. Both can be found in art supply stores.

Sandpaper, steel wool, and aluminum scourers have lots of uses. They are great for correcting small mistakes when painting, for scoring surfaces and getting them ready for further coats of paint, as well as for scarring them to create the effect of age. The texture of these materials varies from very coarse to extra-fine. There are also abrasives available for wood, metal, and for using wet to create fine finishes.

When painting, and especially when working on a scaffolding or a tall ladder for any length of time, a vest or apron with pockets for holding the things you are using, such as paintbrushes, paints, rags, and other items, is very handy and saves time and energy.

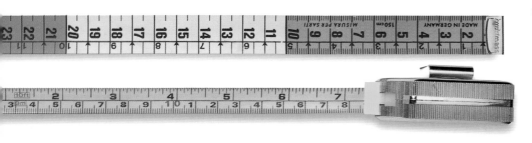

Materials for preparing surfaces

The preparation of surfaces to be decorated must be done carefully. The success of a project depends on the quality of preparation, the stencil design, and the care taken to protect and finish the surface of the design. Once the surface has been prepared, it is a good idea to put aside some of the paint for correcting mistakes that may occur while stenciling.

Paints for priming surfaces

The aim of painting is to protect, and at the same time decorate, surfaces. The quality of a paint is measured by its yield, its covering capacity, and the length of time it will keep both its protective qualities and the intensity of its color. Yield refers to the number of square feet that can be painted with one gallon (3.8L) of paint. Its durability depends to a great degree on the preparation and the state of the surface, on the quality of the paint applied, and on the technique of application.

In order to obtain a long-lasting surface with a good finish, keep in mind the painting procedures discussed on page 24. When priming, make sure that the surface to be painted is porous and perfectly clean.

In general, it is better to apply two or three thin coats of paint than one thick one, especially with oil paints. The first coat should be thinner or slightly diluted with solvent so that the paint penetrates well into the surface, forming a suitable base to which subsequent coats will adhere. Later applications may be thicker.

Just as with the paints for stenciling, paints for priming the surface can be water or oil based. Plastic or acrylic gloss paints are water based. Synthetic enamel paints or semilacquers are oil based. Both are washable.

Oil paint or oil-based enamels are best for painting wood furniture, floors, doors, and windows.

Plastic paint is suitable for interior walls.

The new generation of all-purpose paints can be used to paint all kinds of surfaces that do not allow the paint to adhere well, such as Formica and plastic. Although it usually comes in white, it can be colored with pigment.

Acrylic gloss is recommended for indoor painting such as kitchens and bathrooms. It is also suitable as an exterior paint.

Paints for priming surfaces

Type	Applications	Can be stenciled with	Solvent
• Matte or gloss plastic-based (acrylic) paint	• Water-based acrylic or plastic paints for all interior walls. Matte is recommended for damaged or uneven walls, gloss for very smooth, even walls.	• Acrylic or oil paints	• Water
• Acrylic glosses	• Water-based plastic paints for interior and exterior walls. Highly recommended for damp areas such as bathrooms and kitchens, which will nicely take a glossy finish.	• Acrylic or oil paints, or synthetic enamels	• Water
• Synthetic enamels, matte, gloss, or brilliant	• Oil-based paint. Suitable for windows, doors, furniture, and wood and cork floors.	• Synthetic oils and enamels	• Paint thinner or turpentine
• All-purpose paints	• Surfaces with adherence problems, like Formica, plastic, and other nonporous surfaces.	• Acrylic paints	• Water

Materials for finishing and surface protection

Brushes for varnish should be thick and long bristled (triple or quadruple brushes), and should be very soft in order to take up and leave the right amount of varnish. They must be clean and free from dust.

Many stenciled decorations need to be covered with a finishing layer to protect and ensure permanence. In general, this does not apply to walls but to decorative objects and furniture, which should be protected using varnish or wax. These, used together with patinas of various kinds, also enrich the look of objects and give quality to the finish.

Varnishes

Varnish serves two purposes: On the one hand, it protects the piece from possible damage due to scraping, temperature variation, dust, humidity, light, and bruising, and on the other hand, it improves the object's finish, adding a rich quality to its appearance. Varnishes also can be water based or oil based. Acrylic varnishes are water based and, therefore are suitable for preserving pieces decorated only with water-based colors. Synthetic and polyurethane varnishes are oil based and protect pieces painted with *either* water- or oil-based paints.

• Acrylic varnishes

Acrylic varnishes are water based and come in gloss or matte finish. They are quite damage-resistant and can be washed. They do not fade with time and are quick-drying, requiring about two hours between coats. To obtain a finer finish, smoothing bubbles and pockmarks, use wet-type sandpaper and a little water mixed with liquid detergent.

• Synthetic varnishes

Synthetic varnishes are oil based and are diluted with turpentine. They can be gloss or matte. They yellow somewhat with time and so may alter colors, especially blues, but even this effect can be attractive. They are very resilient and are most suitable for indoor use. To obtain a smooth, fine finish, the coat of varnish is sanded with wet-type sandpaper.

• Polyurethane varnishes

Polyurethane varnishes are oil based and can be gloss or matte. They are extremely resilient and are most suitable for outdoor use and for floors. They turn somewhat yellow like all oil-based varnishes. They are washable and do not deteriorate, although they may crack with sudden temperature changes. They are very tough to smooth down so it will be necessary to use different grades of wet-type sandpaper to get rid of bubbles and imperfections.

Synthetic varnish *(Fig. 1)*. Polyurethane varnish *(Fig. 2)*. Acrylic varnish *(Fig. 3)*.

Waxes

Applying a wax finish is a traditional method of protecting and improving the look of wood. A wax finish gives a certain natural look that improves with use and, at the same time, nourishes the fibers of the wood. The most frequently used waxes are beeswax and carnauba wax. You will find many kinds of waxes, both colorless and dyed, in stores specializing in wood treatment. The use of wax is recommended for pieces that do not require a tough final coat or the luster of varnish. When applied to the inside of drawers or wardrobes, the fragrance mingles with the natural smell of the wood.

Instead of varnishing, pieces can also be waxed. However, wax does not protect as well as varnish does, so it is better to wax after varnishing. Wax is applied with a grade 0000 steel wool pad. After the wax dries it should be buffed and polished with a soft cotton rag.

Aged finishes and patinas

An aged finish adds charm and beauty to an object. Included next is a list of materials for obtaining the effects of wear, crackling, and aging that appear on furniture over the years. This is one of the most attractive finishes for the application of stenciling.

Aging techniques consist of imitating the wear and tear that alters a piece of furniture over many years, due to the effects of light, dampness, rubbing, dirt, and use in general. The effects of time cause paint to fade or darken, to crackle or flake. With sandpaper and steel wool, you can transform a recently finished stenciled piece, giving it the look of an antique.

With special varnishes for crackling, you can imitate the cracks produced on painted surfaces due, for instance, to sudden temperature changes. Once the effect has been achieved, a dark patina is applied that highlights these cracks and crevices. "Patina" refers to the layer of dirt and accumulation and color alteration, the result of time and wear and tear on the surface of an object. A subtle patina is pleasant to look at and can give added richness to a stencil, adding to the charm of the piece. Special products are available to create this effect, such as waxes dyed with the colors of different types of wood. Another way of coloring wax is to stain colorless wax with oil paint. All of these are easy to apply and will create attractive patinas.

The use of patinas and techniques for aging is not restricted to wood. Any stenciled surface can be aged, except fabrics. Patinas, like wax, represent the final step in decorating.

White wax, which is actually colorless, can be applied to all surfaces without altering the surface's color. Yellow wax is an antique dealers' wax that is suitable for any surface, although it is specially recommended for old furniture because it nourishes wood dried with age. It is usually composed of several waxes including carnauba and beeswax. Mahogany-colored wax is used for surfaces painted with earth colors, reds, and terra-cottas. In addition, there are walnut- and oak-colored waxes, and a variety of others.

The most effective materials for creating the look of age are steel wool pads, both fine and coarse, for "spoiling" or scarring the stenciled design, and colored waxes. There are other oils, varnishes, and various commercial patinas that are now widely sold.

Varnishes for obtaining cracked finishes.

Green sandpaper is the most suitable type for sanding down natural wood before applying a first coat of paint. Black sandpaper or emery cloth is wet sandpaper (sandpaper that can be used with water) and is suitable for painted or varnished surfaces. When dampened, this paper will create a fine surface without raising dust. Sanding sponges are easy to use as they fit into the palm of your hand, allow you to apply uniform pressure, and can adapt to awkward edges such as those in moldings and corners.

Cleaning and conserving of materials

Cleaning your materials immediately after use will be easy and quick. If they are left for long, it may be too late, as the materials used are often permanent. Aggressive methods will be needed to eliminate dried varnish or paint. As a consequence, stencils and applicators may deteriorate. Bear in mind that well-cared-for materials will last for years.

Cleaning and conserving stencils

The great advantage of stenciling rather than freehand painting is that the cut-out design can be repeated an infinite number of times on an enormous variety of surfaces. So that they do not lose their shape and precision, it is important to clean stencils as thoroughly as possible and store them carefully. A large collection of stencils can become a significant technical aid and a rich source of design creativity.

How to clean stencils

Polyester paper stencils should be cleaned and left until completely dry before putting them away. To clean them, lay them out on a sheet of paper and clean them with water or turpentine, depending on the type of paint used.

Here the paint used was oil based: First the paint is removed from the stencil using turpentine. It is then cleaned with a sponge and liquid detergent and rinsed in hot water.

Water-based paint has been used here. The stencils are wiped gently with a sponge and a little liquid detergent. If the paint is very dry, a smooth scouring pad or cloth may be used. Stencils should not be scrubbed vigorously as the design may be damaged. The stencil is then rinsed in hot water. The operation is repeated if necessary until the paint has been completely removed. Finally, the stencils are allowed to dry before storing.

How to store stencils

Polyester paper stencils are fairly strong and durable. To ensure their long life, they must be stored so that they do not get dusty or creased. They can be kept in folders, plastic bags, or envelopes, and hung in a cupboard or from a coat hanger.

Since manila paper stencils cannot be washed with water, other measures must be taken to conserve their designs. With frequent handling, manila paper stencils also get torn, or accumulated paint distorts the shapes of the design. The most effective way of conserving them is to duplicate them on another piece of manila paper. To accomplish this, the worn stencil is placed over a fresh piece of manila paper and paint is sprayed onto the design. In this way, the stencil is perfectly reproduced on a new surface and it will be necessary only to cut out the design the next time it is needed.

Before a stencil is stored, it should be checked to see that the paint is completely dry. Aerosol enamels and oil-based paints take longer to dry than water-based paints. As paper stencils are easily damaged, they should be kept flat in a box, with paper between them. Coating them with talcum powder will keep tacky surfaces from sticking.

Once a stencil has deteriorated, the design is duplicated on a clean sheet of manila paper with the same aerosol used for painting.

Lay your stencils flat, and dust with a light coat of talcum powder to prevent them from sticking together. Cover each with a sheet of paper, then place the next stencil on top to store.

Large stencils or multiple stencils for a single design can be easily stored in plastic bags and then hung up. Transparent bags make the stencils easy to find.

Cleaning applicators

Paintbrushes are the only applicators that need to be cleaned since both sponges and rollers usually become so coated with dry paint that they generally cannot be reused.

It is best not to let paintbrushes dry out completely as dry paint is difficult to remove. Sometimes it is possible to soften paint that has dried by using one of the cleaning products available on the market.

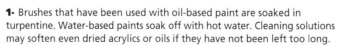

1- Brushes that have been used with oil-based paint are soaked in turpentine. Water-based paints soak off with hot water. Cleaning solutions may soften even dried acrylics or oils if they have not been left too long.

2- Brushes are lathered with hot water and liquid or solid soap and worked against a rough surface in a circular motion. Once all residue of the paint has been completely removed, brushes are rinsed until the soap is washed out and the water runs clear.

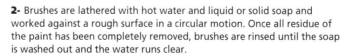

3- Paintbrushes are laid on an absorbent surface to dry. This will help to conserve the shape of the brush and allow the piece joining the handle to dry.

4- The use of a hair dryer will speed the process along. This leaves the bristles soft, but too much heat may cause the handle to split.

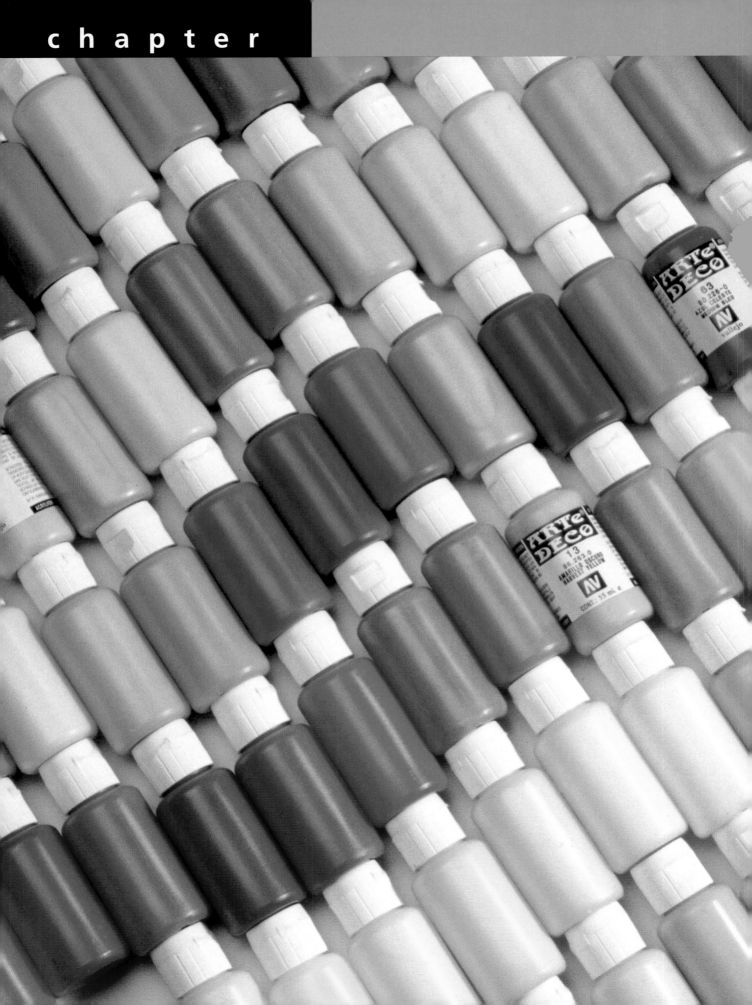

Painting with stencils and choosing colors

The facility for creating original, attractive, well-designed, and well-executed stencil decorations for an infinite variety of surfaces and spaces is the mark of a stencil artist. Stenciling is a simple, rewarding technique. To become a competent stencil artist, you do not need any special artistic ability, but you do need to know the method thoroughly to use it well. In this chapter we will discuss the basic and key points of effective stenciling. Methods used for creating stenciled designs as well as the reasoning behind their use will be presented, with special emphasis on the use of a variety of applicators and paints. The information in this chapter will give you a firm grounding in techniques and equip you for tackling even the most challenging of projects.

Methods of stenciling with a paintbrush

Traditional ways of applying paint with a stenciling brush are the circular method and the stippling method. The former is the most frequently used in England, and the latter in the United States. Each method can be combined with the other, although each will create a different finish. The best idea is to experiment with each of these methods to see which will work best for the job to be done. Both methods can be used for any of the paints discussed.

Circular motion method

This method consists of painting in circles with the paintbrush held perpendicular to the surface, containing only a small amount of paint so that the strokes are very dry. The paint dries almost immediately, so successive layers and shading can follow fairly quickly. The circular method is characterized by its very hazy and transparent finish, with subtle and well-graded shadows. This method of stenciling is especially suitable for use when you want to obtain images that appear aged. It can also be used to create the illusion of three dimensions, as it will depict depth and allow you to create very-well-graded shadows for realistic-looking results.

The color of the background surface plays an important role in stenciling, as it will be the principal color with which all others will interact.

Circular brushstroking can be carried out on porous or matte surfaces. This is a good method for decorating children's bedrooms, old furniture and other objects, and unvarnished wood, and it can be highly refined for rich and subtle effects.

Using the circular motion method, smooth and transparent finishes can be achieved, as well as delicately fading shadows.

Stippling method

The stippling method consists of applying the paint while holding the paintbrush perpendicular to the surface, then lightly dabbing through the shapes cut out of the stencil. Here, too, the paintbrush should not carry too much paint, although a little more than with circular motion painting. Because more paint is used, the drying time is a little longer between layers. The force with which you use the brush will determine how opaque the stenciled design will be. With more paint and more force, it will be denser; with less paint and a more gentle application, the result will be more transparent.

Stippling is characterized by its thicker appearance, having more volume and texture. The final result is more intense and less transparent than in the circular method. For this reason, instead of creating a three-dimensional illusion, stippled stencils have the look of superimposed color and paint. The shadows are not so hazy and delicate. A certain amount of practice is needed to learn to achieve well-blended shadows using this method.

With stippling, the base color of your surface is less important, as the marks are more opaque and compact, and may even cover the base color completely.

This is a good method for painting on surfaces that are not too porous and are painted with glossy oil paint, varnished, rough, or textured. Stippling is also a good method for decorating areas that need strong images or contrasts. It tends to be decorative, creating flat images that have the look of having been printed, rather than modeling a realistic form.

By stippling gently with the paintbrush, we can obtain textured and dense finishes.

How to organize your work space

To paint in comfort, the work space should be well lit, with materials organized and within easy reach. A big worktable is ideal; a small ladder with an auxiliary tray support or a cart on wheels can also be used. Both the table and the tray should be protected with paper. Your stencils can be stuck with masking or drafting tape to a window or to the edges of the table so they do not get in the way when painting. Besides a palette, plastic or old china plates can be used to hold paint.

Painting with liquid paints

Liquid paints have a consistency similar to thin, somewhat watery cream. Acrylic paints fall into this group. Acrylics come in tubes or wide-mouthed glass or plastic jars. When they come into contact with the air, they rapidly lose their consistency and dry out. As it is very important to maintain a constant consistency through the duration of your project, you must take care to keep acrylics from drying out. Stenciling is, in general, a dry brush technique, which means that when painting, the paintbrush should carry a minimum amount of paint.

To carry out these first practice exercises, we advise using watercolor paper or paper with a matte, absorbent finish.

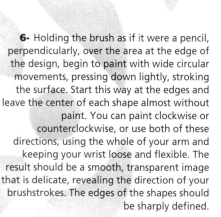

Liquid paints.

1- First, hold the stencil up, away from your surface, while spraying it with a spray adhesive.

2- Press the stencil to your paper or surface, making sure that it is completely flat.

3- Deposit a little liquid paint on the palette or other paint receptacle. The wide lids of liquid paint jars can be put to use to hold the paint as well.

4- With a thoroughly dry brush, held perpendicular to the surface, place the tips of the bristles in the paint and pick up a small amount of color, no more than covering the flat part of the bristles.

6- Holding the brush as if it were a pencil, perpendicularly, over the area at the edge of the design, begin to paint with wide circular movements, pressing down lightly, stroking the surface. Start this way at the edges and leave the center of each shape almost without paint. You can paint clockwise or counterclockwise, or use both of these directions, using the whole of your arm and keeping your wrist loose and flexible. The result should be a smooth, transparent image that is delicate, revealing the direction of your brushstrokes. The edges of the shapes should be sharply defined.

5- Unload the paint from the brush by rubbing vigorously on a paper napkin or other thick absorbent paper, until the brush is practically dry. Excess paint produces blotches that are difficult to hide. You also risk having the paint slide under the edges of the stencil, blurring the work.

Painting with solid paints

Solid paints have a compact consistency. They can be water or oil based, and come as creams or in sticks. They are very manageable for beginners, since they naturally solve some typical problems, such as too much paint on the brush, and slippage and bleeding of paint under the edges of the stencil, marring and smudging the decorated surface.

Paints in sticks

These paints take the shape of thick pencils, and like wax crayons, they are protected with a width of paper and have a compact consistency. Paint sticks are oil based and so are cleaned with paint thinner or turpentine, and like oil paints, they are slower-drying than acrylics. There are oil sticks that are made for stenciling but sticks meant for painting can be used in the same way. They should not be used directly on the surface to be decorated, however. The stick is the paint's container and the color is first deposited on a nonabsorbent surface or palette.

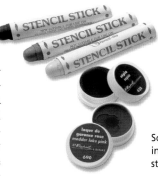

Solid paints come in creams or sticks.

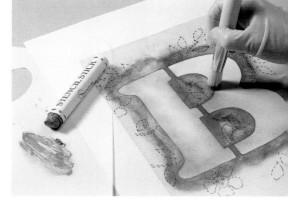

1- The color is applied by rubbing the stick directly onto a nonabsorbent surface, a sheet of glass, or, as shown here, a disposable paper palette.

2- With paint in stick form, it is practically impossible to pick up more paint on your brush than you need so paper or absorbent toweling is not needed to dry the bristles. The brush is held like a pencil and a small amount of paint is picked up with a circular motion to cover the tips of the bristles evenly.

3- With the paintbrush held perpendicularly over the stencil, begin to paint using circular motions, working from the edges to the center of your shape and pressing gently.

Paints in cream form

Their consistency is similar to creamy face makeup. They are made by various manufacturers, may be water based or oil based, and will need the appropriate solvent: water or turpentine. They come in wide-mouthed plastic containers. When opening one of these for the first time, it is necessary to remove the protective cellophane that covers its surface. Some paints are self-sealing, which means that, if they are not in use for a period of time, a fine film will form over the surface of the paint that functions to prevent the paint from drying out. The look and quality of stenciling done with creams closely resembles that of paint in sticks.

1. With the brush held perpendicularly, dip it into the surface of the paint, using it straight from the pot.

2. Then distribute it over the bristles on clean, absorbent paper, paper towel, or on the stenciled design itself.

3. Paint in a circular motion.

There is no need to pour the paint out onto your palette, as small quantities can be used directly from the pot. As these paints do not contain excess water, it is not necessary to remove excess paint with a paper towel. An image that has been stenciled with cream paints, as with paint sticks, has a smooth, fine look. The design in the photograph has been done with both types of paint and the results are practically the same.

Problems and solutions

Although stenciling is a simple technique, trial and error are required for its mastery. A great deal of the charm of stenciling is its handmade look and the nuance and delicacy of its shading. Mistakes and imperfections are part of its creativity and often add to its beauty. Some mistakes, however, may need correction.

Insufficient paint

A common error when you are just starting out is to use too much paint or too little. When the paint spreads or bleeds under the edges of the stencil, it means that the brush is holding too much paint. As a precautionary measure, before starting to paint, you should always rub the brush vigorously on a piece of paper towel to remove the excess paint.

Another common mistake is to alter the consistency of the paint as you work. Take care to dry off excess paint each time you dip your brush in paint, thus ensuring a uniform consistency.

In this case, too little paint has been used. The result is dull and lifeless.

This is the result of using paint that is too dry and lumpy. The circular motions of the paintbrush are too visible.

An excess of paint has caused it to run slightly under the stencil *(A)*. The best solution, if the blot is not too big, is to replace the stencil on the painted design, move it slightly so that the edge of the shape exposes the area where the paint has bled, then paint over the imperfection to cover it *(B)*.

A

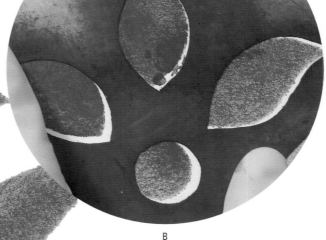

B

Your work is covered with dust

This is a common problem when using liquid acrylic paints and is due to an excessive buildup of dry paint on the paintbrush. To avoid this problem, you must make sure that your paintbrush remains moist throughout the work.

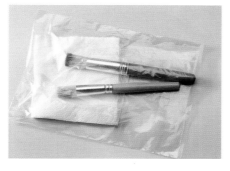

It is important to make sure that your paintbrush is always moist. A good way to do this is to wet a paper towel and put it into a plastic bag. Each time you have to stop work, put the brush into the bag and close it. This will keep your brush moist and the paint from drying out.

When the paint on your brush has become dry, it will encourage the accumulation of fine specks of dust.

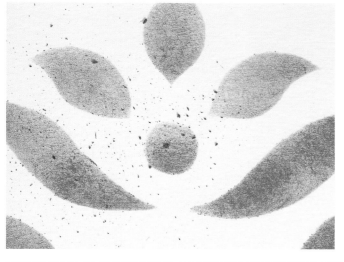

The solution is to go back over the surface of your paint with a soft, dry brush to remove any dust residue.

The paint loses its consistency

The temperature, the dryness of the atmosphere, interruptions while you are working, or the size of the job can mean that the paint on your palette dries out or loses its liquid consistency. When the paint becomes lumpy or too dry, the surface of your work may be marred as the paintbrush's bristles lose their flexibility. To counter this, use fresh paint on your palette periodically.

1. Shake the paint container well before opening it.

2. Before you begin stenciling, place a small quantity of color on the palette, closing the container immediately so the paint doesn't lose moisture.

3. If the paint dries out and loses its consistency during the course of your work, add one or two drops of slow-drying agent to the paint and mix thoroughly.

Retarding agents that will slow the drying time of paint are transparent. Two or three drops of retarder are enough to bring lumpy paint that has begun to dry out back to its original consistency.

The edges of the stencil have become filled with paint and the design has been greatly altered.

The edges of the stencil have become filled with paint

The problem of too much paint is common when you are stenciling with very small shapes and the design is repeated over a large area. It is important to control the amount of paint on the brush to avoid flooding the design. When this happens, it is advisable to stop your work and get rid of the extra paint by washing the stencil with soap and hot water, a sponge, or a fine scouring pad. Dry it with a lint-free towel or cotton cloth before proceeding with your work.

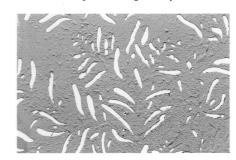

Shading and volume with a brush

A stencil that is flat and opaque gives little suggestion of its potential. Each one of the "cells" contained in a design, connected to the other shapes by "bridges," forms an important part of the whole. From the simplest design to the most challenging, a stencil is alive with possibility.

Shading will give a three-dimensional illusion to its flat shapes, and liven up its color. Thin, dry, transparent colors will give the illusion of volume and shade by building dense areas and overlaying colors.

Shading with the same color

As you will see from the following step-by-step guide, you do not need to mix different tones of the same color in advance, as you can obtain an infinite range of intermediate tones very gradually by going over a previously painted area several times with the same color. In general, you should shade from a light color to a darker one. In the instructions that follow we will demonstrate the circular method of shading. The same skills can also be applied to the stippled method.

1- **The first color gradation.** Paint the shapes, in the chosen color, using the technique that has been previously explained (see page 36), starting with the edges and very gently moving to the center, leaving a small central part sparsely painted, with much of the background showing through. You can immediately see the first suggestions of shading at the edges and more strongly in the darker shapes. The very small shapes should be lightly painted, filling in the shape completely.

2- **The second color gradation.** Without lifting up the stencil, go back over the edges using circular motions, and press down harder on the brush. Cover about a third of the previously painted area, preserving the lighter color of the central area of each shape. In this way, an intermediate tone has been created.

3- **The third color gradation.** With a small paintbrush and the same color paint, go over the edges without completely covering the previous gradation. The more you brush over the same area, the darker the color will get. This last stage can be done using the stippled method to finish with a layer of more intense color. The result is a design that moves and shimmers with tones of the same color.

Shading by layering colors

Stenciled designs are even more beautiful if, in addition to grading with different tones of the same color, their volumes are defined in a more elaborate and expressive way by using several colors. Some shapes will be made up of several colors, the pears, apples, and leaves, for instance, which will add to the illusion of volume. Superimposing color over color creates new colors, mixtures that may not be available commercially. If you paint in a very transparent way, layering several colors, you can achieve some unique and beautiful visual mixtures. For example, layering red over yellow gives orange; blue over yellow, green; green over red, brown.

The following step-by-step guide will offer examples using this type of shading. We have used the same design as in the previous example so that you can see the difference between them, and because its subject and forms lend themselves to color representation.

1- All the shapes have been painted very lightly with a pale, transparent base color.

2- First layer. The shapes are graded with natural colors but in a medium tone. It is essential to paint maintaining the transparency of the color so that the base color is not completely covered.

3- Second layer. The edges and some shapes—in this case, the pears, which in reality have brown spots—are graded with a darker color and tone than at first, making sure that the previously applied colors are not hidden. The resulting composition has a vibrancy of color that can be achieved only by this kind of color layering.

As you look at this still life, notice the subtle and varied coloration of the fruit, glowing with visual mixtures.

The first layer of paint colors the pear. The yellow base color has been followed with a green layer, and then a red; the result is a brownish red. The second layer of color is for the leaves. On an egg-yellow base we have superimposed layers of green. The result is a warm green. The third layer of paint colors the grapes. Red has been layered over blue, resulting in purple.

Other color applicators

Many stenciled designs are done with a paintbrush; however, you can achieve interesting results by using other modes of application as well. The success of these alternative methods depends, though, on the degree of facility you gain with the paintbrush. Stencils that have been done with a sponge roller, sponge, or with an aerosol spray are very different in effect from paintbrush stenciling but no less attractive. A variety of applicators can also be combined to achieve very creative effects, altering the rhythms of the different textures and densities. Experimenting with these as well as other materials for paint application is well worth the time and effort and is bound to yield creative results.

Stenciling with a sponge roller

A high-density synthetic sponge roller makes an excellent stenciling tool, but can be used only with liquid paints. As the roller absorbs much more paint than other applicators, it is important to allow for more paint for each project. This means that the work may be a little more costly, but you will economize on time. A sponge roller is extremely useful for painting a large area of background color quickly, reducing the time spent on a long project. This type of roller will also paint consistently uniform transparency. Interchangeable rollers of many different sizes can be readily purchased for use with one handle. The best size is the one that fits your design: If the roller is too small, you may get seam lines made by its outer edges; if it is too big, you will likely paint outside the limits of the stencil.

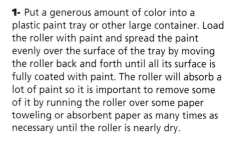

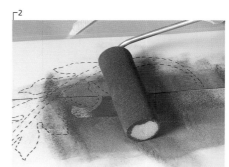

1- Put a generous amount of color into a plastic paint tray or other large container. Load the roller with paint and spread the paint evenly over the surface of the tray by moving the roller back and forth until all its surface is fully coated with paint. The roller will absorb a lot of paint so it is important to remove some of it by running the roller over some paper toweling or absorbent paper as many times as necessary until the roller is nearly dry.

2- Using a moderate amount of pressure, apply the paint to the design beginning lengthwise, painting in one direction and then in the other. Never use small dabs as this will lead to awkward concentrations of color or shading.

3- A roller is a useful tool for painting monochromatic designs on large surfaces. Once you have applied the base color, you can add layers of shading with a paintbrush or a synthetic sponge, applying the same color repeatedly at the edges.

Stenciling with synthetic sponge or foam rubber

This is a good method for producing shading, for use with metal stencils, or for designs that consist of very small shapes. It is not the best way to approach larger projects, however, as it is a much slower process than working with a brush or roller.

The sponge, glued to its small cylindrical applicator that comprises a roller, can be used on its side as a stamper, or you can make stampers by cutting up small pieces of foam rubber or high-density synthetic sponge. You can use these with any kind of paint.

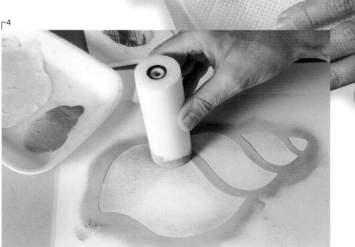

1- Once the color has been put into the tray or other container, wet the flat part or side of the piece of sponge with some of the paint, without exerting too much pressure, and then stamp with it.

2- Remove the excess paint on absorbent paper or paper toweling.

3- Stencil with small, soft dabs through the cut-out shapes, working from the edges toward the center and leaving this part without any color, in the same way as when painting with a brush, always remembering that a stenciled image should look soft and transparent.

4- The look of the printed design depends upon the density of the sponge used. It is interesting to practice with different densities to see the effects they create. To add tints or to achieve shades and depth, you have to dab the edges of your shapes with the same color. To increase the density of the color, add layers of color, repeating the previous steps as often as necessary. Try to avoid compacted and wet spots.

5- The end result is an attractive design with intense and compact, rather than transparent, colors, which is strong and very effective, particularly on rustic or old-looking surfaces. Its finish is made up of an infinity of small dots that mix when viewed at a certain distance, giving vibrancy and shimmer to the color.

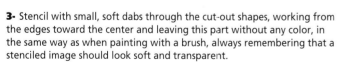

Stenciling with an aerosol

A spray paint can be either water and plastic based or oil-based enamel. Either one of these, as well as aerosol sprays, which are sold to touch up the body of a car, can be used. Just take into account their different drying times. Manila paper and cardboard are surfaces that will accept these paints. When applied to polyester papers, the paint will slip and can stain the rest of the design. Given that this technique is more difficult to control, it is a good idea to experiment first to get an idea of the potential strengths and problems of paints and surfaces you are working with.

It is important to read the manufacturer's instructions to know which kind of paint you should use and which is its appropriate solvent, water or turpentine. Depending on whether it is water or oil based, its drying time will be faster or slower. Bear in mind that water-based paint cannot be used to decorate surfaces painted with an oil-based product. It is also advisable to wear a face mask when using an aerosol as it is very easy to inhale its extremely fine paint particles, which tend to be toxic. Stenciling with an aerosol is ideal for walls and floors because it is very fast and uniform. All it takes is a little experience in its application. Also, you can achieve tints and shades by spraying with different layers of colors that can add a great chromatic richness. You can then use a fine aluminum scouring pad to soften the stenciled image so that it acquires a more subtle finished result.

Shading with three-layered colors from dark to light

Up to now we have been shading from light to dark, but with aerosol paint, you can also shade from dark to light to create subtle mixtures of colors, leaving the lights or shine to be done on the upper, or last, layer.

1- With the aid of a squared mask held parallel with your work surface and placed to protect areas of your design, shade very lightly with green.

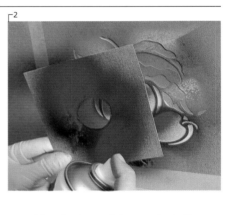

2- With a circular mask for creating half-moon shadows, easily made using circular shapes, paint with red.

3- With a very small, circle-shaped mask, very useful for creating effects of light, spray with yellow onto the leaves and fruit, creating glints of light.

4- The result of this sort of layering of light colors over dark colors is a rich chromatic image. In this photograph, you can see the way it has constructed the volume of the fruit.

Masks

The aerosol's nozzle allows the paint to spray at quite a wide angle. In order to be able to guide and control its coverage of a precise area, and to avoid unwanted paint mixing, it is essential to use masks. Shown here are pieces of cardboard that are cut to various sizes.

Masks cut with a small round hole are used to shade small shapes such as grapes and strawberries; those with a square hole are useful for corners.

1- Protect the area surrounding your design with paper. Fix the stencil to the surface with a spray-on adhesive. It should lie completely flat, without any puckers or warps, and well adhered to the surface so that the paint cannot slide or bleed underneath. Secure the edges with masking or drafting tape.

2- Shake the can well before painting and be sure the nozzle is clear by spraying onto a piece of cardboard. The spray should be uniform and without any drips. When you have finished, turn the can upside down and spray for a few seconds until the paint stops coming out.

3- Spray with short, sharp bursts at a distance of about 5 to 8 inches (13 to 20 cm) from the surface for large areas and light coloring and at 3 to 4 inches (8 to 10 cm) for details, small shapes, and more intense tones.
With the can slightly angled, spray for about one or two seconds using uniform up-and-down motions so that there is no accumulation of excess paint at the edges, which may slide underneath and mar your design.

4- Use the masks to create shading, directing the sprayed paint and avoiding the mixing of unwanted color. Hold a piece of cardboard and cover the areas you do not wish to shade, then spray. Now, move the mask to the next shape, continuing with this process until the work is completed.

5- The result is an image with intense, lively color. Stencils sprayed with aerosol paints read beautifully from a distance, producing some wonderful effects. Notice the way some areas have blended with ocher, while others have retained their blue color.

Color

Stenciling is characterized by its soft, pastel, transparent colors. A stenciled image gives the impression that it is emerging from the surface onto which it is painted. It is not particularly important whether the colors are dark or light. What is important is that they are not only uniform and flat, but also vary in tone, density, color intensity, and rhythm, giving them the charming look of hand painting rather than mass production. Stenciling has many looks to it, using subtle tones and strong contrasts. Both simpler and more complex patterns will produce attractive results.

How to choose the color

The colors for your design should be used in the spirit of exploration, as is appropriate for working out any piece of art. Watch the effect of color as you paint with it and what pleases your eye. It is this experience that should determine the colors you choose from the extremely wide range offered by paint manufacturers.

Sometimes, one has an innate sense of color, its mixtures, and its combinations, but more often a good color sense is acquired with experience. It is hard to generalize about color as each person has his or her own unique color sense. Color surrounds us in every aspect of daily life; it takes an awareness of color to notice and appreciate its presence. All the colors in the natural world, as well as the patterns on all the objects that surround us, continually stimulate our senses. Stopping for a moment to notice these colors, observing them with a critical eye, is the beginning of color awareness. From this first analysis to falling in love with a color or a specific combination of colors, your own sense of what is beautiful must become your guide to its use and enjoyment.

This collection of fruit is a treat for our eyes. Pausing for a moment to take in its beauty, or standing before a landscape or sunset and letting the colors invade your senses, is an important personal experience that will guide you to choose the colors you will later use for your decorations.

Cool and warm colors

Cool colors can be quiet and subtle in wall decoration. They can suggest depth and create volume, visually transforming a space. Cool colors include blues, grays, and violets.

Warm colors are cheerful and welcoming; they tend to dominate rather than play a quiet, secondary role. They have a greater intensity than cool colors, give a sense of light, and produce an effect of closeness. Reds, oranges, and yellows are all warm colors.

Though cools and warms have particular characteristics, it is possible to modify these by mixing. If blue is mixed with red or orange, it will become a warm blue. In the same way, if red is mixed with violet or crimson, it will become a cool red.

This blue wall is part of an office. It offers a calm, relaxing work atmosphere.

This wall that is painted in a warm off-white and stenciled with red ocher livens up a hallway in a home.

Clean or aged colors

Clean colors are those that do not contain any brown in their composition; adding some brown to color will give the illusion of its aging. Choosing one or the other effect depends on the characteristics of your surface and the look you want to heighten or create. The most suitable colors for a child's bedroom, for instance, are clean, pastel colors. Very often, however, aged, tinted colors define the charm that characterizes stenciled surfaces.

Here, pure blues and yellows have been used to achieve a cheery image. The color is transparent and clean.

Tinted and aged-looking colors have been used here to stencil a vine and grapes, lending this kitchen an Old World look.

Mixtures of color

Why do we have to mix colors if we can find an extremely wide range of colors on the market? As stenciling is a decorative finish, you will want to adapt its colors to its setting. It is difficult to find a commercial color that is exactly the one you want. In general, too, commercial colors tend to be excessively defined, so for this reason you will most often want to mix your own.

A suitable mixture substantially enriches any work and, at the same time, gives it the charm and originality that each person brings to it.

Every year new pigments and variations of color come onto the market. Even with such wide ranges to choose from, however, you will often find it necessary to mix your own.

Primary colors

The study of colors has, for a long time, been centered on the idea that you can mix all the colors of the spectrum and their different tones from three primary colors: magenta, yellow, and blue. These are elemental, pure colors that cannot be obtained by mixing. A design may require only small amounts of the primary colors in their pure form.

A chromatic circle with the primary colors, blue, magenta, and yellow. These colors cannot be obtained by mixing.

Secondary colors

The three secondary colors are obtained by mixing pairs of primary colors, so, by mixing magenta with yellow, you get orange; a yellow and dark blue mix results in green; violet or dark purple results from mixing dark blue with magenta. Variations of the color depend on the quantity of the pigments mixed.

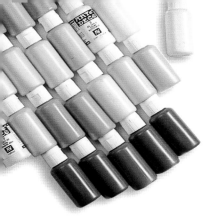

Complementary colors

Complementary colors, placed side by side, produce strong contrasts. The three pairs of complementary colors are: orange and blue, green and red, yellow and purple. Complementary colors are mixed, rather than elemental, colors. They further mix the tertiary colors: yellow-green, yellow-orange, red-orange, red-violet, blue-violet, and blue-green. You can obtain an extremely interesting and extensive array of other colors, as well. The addition of white and black to your palette will also greatly increase your color range.

Complementary colors are opposite the primary colors in the chromatic circle, or color wheel.

Black and white

Starting from the mixture of secondary colors, and with different amounts of white or black, you can obtain a range of pastel and grayish colors. Too much black muddies color. To lighten or change a color into a pastel, you will need liberal amounts of white, so you will find it useful to have white on hand in quantities at least double the amount of your other colors.

Chromatic circle of the secondary colors obtained when the primary colors are mixed together.

Gray colors are obtained here by mixing black with the secondary colors.

The same colors when mixed with white. The results are the pastel colors.

Designing and making the stencils

The choice of a stenciling design suitable to a particular surface is one that will take thought, planning, and some sketching. There will be areas of your surface that need just a decorative touch to finish off a more complex design. Such areas will need to be dealt with differently, perhaps, than the central design. For this reason, you'll need to analyze beforehand the characteristics and requirements of the surface to be decorated, taking into account the full effect you wish to achieve. This chapter will discuss the early planning stages required to design and execute a surface with stenciling. It will cover key sources of ideas and inspiration for designs, and will teach you in detail how to make your own stencils. It is important to choose, at first, projects within your range of skills. The pleasure of stenciling increases progressively as you gain skill and experience over time.

The design of the stencils

Though there is a wide range of styles and motifs of predesigned stencils available on the market, you may not find a design to suit your needs and taste. It will then be necessary to design and make your own stencils.

Designing a stencil project is a creative process, from arriving at an idea, doing sketches, cutting the stencil, working out your color choices, and, finally, stenciling your design in paint on your chosen surface. Seeing the project through from start to finish requires some patience, but will give you great satisfaction.

Materials for making stencils

The materials that are discussed here are those that are the most practical and useful, whether you are skilled at drawing or not. The process is quite doable, for instance, using a simplification of a photocopied design, right through to the cutting out of the stencil.

Tools for drawing stencils

Commercially manufactured technical drawing templates can be very useful for creating your own design. They come in curves, circles, and ellipses that you can trace *(1)*.

A ruler is essential for measuring and for drawing shapes that have straight lines *(2)*.

Tracing paper is useful for reproducing images from a book or photograph to use as designs for stenciling *(3)*.

Graph paper is a good tool for adapting the size of the design to the surface onto which you want to stencil *(4)*.

A pencil is needed for tracing and to work out your sketch or simplify a drawing *(5)*.

Colored pencils are used to experiment with color possibilities as you work out the sketches for your design *(6)*.

Tracing paper pad is useful to simplify the drawing and to try out different ways of adapting the shapes until the design looks the way you want it to *(7)*.

A permanent marker pen is a good tool for copying the design, and registration marks (if you use them), onto the stencil paper, as it will not rinse off when you wash the stencil. It is a good idea to have these in different colors and thicknesses, though you will probably use one with a fine tip most of the time *(8)*.

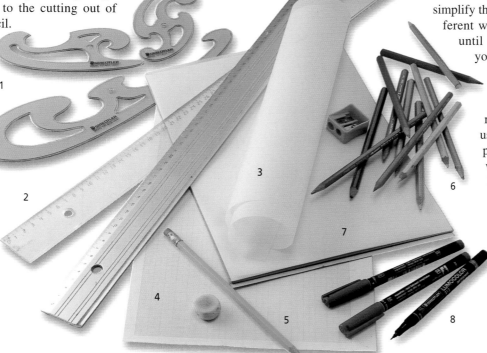

1

2

3

4

5

6

7

8

Tools for cutting out stencils

A craft knife, an X-acto, or a utility knife are all good tools for the precision cutting you will need to do using polyester, manila, or waxed paper, all papers that are used to make stencils. These knives must be very sharp to cut cleanly and the handle should be thick enough to hold comfortably in your hand. X-acto tools have a variety of interchangeable blades, in which case it is a good idea to have several available to use for different sizes and shapes of designs. Utility knives come with continuous blades that are sharpened by breaking off the used piece with a pair of pliers *(1)*.

A metal ruler is very useful for cutting precise, straight shapes *(2)*.

Small curved scissors are a good alternative when a craft knife would be too difficult to use *(3)*.

A cutting mat is used so that you do not destroy or scratch the surface of furniture while cutting your stencils. A glass surface is used when using an electric cutter *(4)*.

An electric cutter is another option, a good tool for beginners, although it can produce some rough edges and should be limited to cutting polyester paper. Use glass, as this cutter works by using heat and would burn other surfaces. During work interruptions, it should be rested on a heat-resistant support *(5)*.

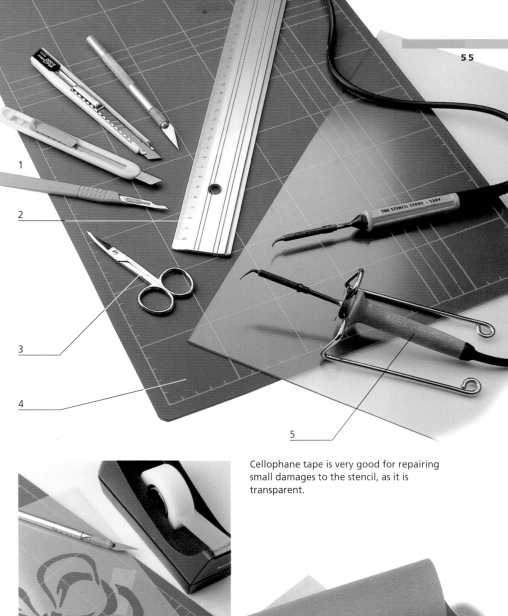

Cellophane tape is very good for repairing small damages to the stencil, as it is transparent.

Polyester paper, waxed cardboard, acetate, and manila paper are sold in rolls or different-sized sheets. The sheets are preferable. Once you have chosen the size of the design, you should buy sheets that best adapt to its measurements. The thickness of the paper you use should be substantial enough to maintain rigidity while remaining flexible.

Choosing the design

Long before taking your paintbrush in hand, you will want to plan and design exactly what you are going to do. The structure of your area and its surroundings may suggest or inspire a design style, such as a frieze, a centralized motif, or pictorial design. Stenciling is often a last, finishing touch, and should not detract from the area it decorates. Rather, it should give the area an almost subtle touch, which seems just right. You can begin a design by applying a few stenciled details, then gradually add more elements or motifs. Build your design slowly, making choices as you work.

Sources of inspiration

Current trends in decoration stress personal style and aesthetic preferences. They are eclectic, mixing and adapting many styles, combining style with the individual's unique feelings, tastes, and vision. Stenciling is one way to introduce such unique elements, allowing you to express your own creativity and add it to your environment.

To find inspiration and sources on which to base your stencil designs, visually assess the space the work will decorate. Almost any element in a particular environment can become the basis of a stencil project.

Elaborating on an existing design

Often, rich sources of inspiration can be found in the features that already decorate a room or an area. If your room is already decorated or if the decoration of your room has already been determined, and furniture, fabrics, and accessories all purchased, you'll want your stencils to share its motifs and colors. The most practical thing to do then is to adjust the decoration to the design of the wallpaper, the fabric of the curtains or rugs, the molding of the furniture, or the design on a set of china. Then you need only to choose from the wealth of motifs that are most likely present.

This beautiful design is stenciled on the wall of a landing in this Art Deco house.

The design of this white wall frieze, as well as that of the curtains, has been inspired by the engraved motif on the wood of the wardrobe.

An enlarged detail of the above photograph.

Here, inspiration has come from the pattern of the curtains that decorate this young child's room. Its design has been reproduced using stencils.

The design shown above has been combined with these playful bears. This stencil was bought in a crafts shop.

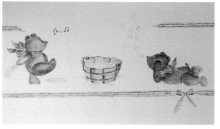

Choosing something new

If the room you wish to decorate has not yet been definitely planned, or if you want to make the stenciled motifs the main focal point of the room, you can turn to other sources of inspiration that don't come from the immediate environment. Here there is no end of possibilities and your own imagination can be your guide. A stencil artist with some experience will welcome the opportunity to combine designs, create original designs, and mix colors, and it is a wonderful opportunity for a beginner to explore.

Inspiration can come from a whole range of sources; designs can be taken from fabric prints, wallpapers, plants, leaves and other natural forms, photos, patterns on china, the pages of art books, wrapping paper patterns, greetings cards, or even children's storybooks.

Whether the designs are inspired by your surroundings or whether they come from other sources, they will need to be adapted to the stenciled image. In the next sections we will discuss the process of adapting a design, transforming it into a mask for stenciling.

The design for this project was inspired by children's stories. An antique doll served as a model for the character of a fairy.

The column painted with characters from children's stories, including Hans Christian Andersen's tale of "The Steadfast Tin Soldier."

What a stencil is like

In chapter 3 you have already worked with a stencil that was precut, so you know what a stenciled image looks like. Before beginning the step-by-step process of designing and cutting out a stencil, it is useful to know a bit more about the parts that make up a stencil and their particular characteristics.

Windows

The window of the stencil is the part that is cut out. This cutout forms the silhouette shape through which color is applied. It is the shape of this window that appears painted on your surface when the stencil is removed. The edges of a window should be carefully shaped and precisely cut out. These window shapes taken together construct the larger image of your stencil, for example, the petals that make up a rose. The shapes are simplified, separated from one another by areas of negative spaces known as "bridges." (See below.)

Notice how the windows of this stencil form the image of a cat. Paint will be applied through these cut-out shapes.

Without the bridges, the cat stencil would be just an empty silhouette. The bridges are placed to deliberately support the design, outlining and shaping the different parts of the animal's body within the stencil.

Bridges

The bridges, or blank spaces that appear around each of the designed shapes, are part of the construction of a stenciled design. Their purpose is to hold the shape, or windows, of the stencil in place and, at the same time, create a space between them. They should be wide enough so that they cannot be easily broken by repeated brushstrokes or washing.

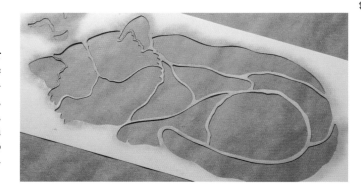

Simple and multiple stencils

A simple stencil is one that has only one color and therefore creates a monochromatic image. The bridges between the shapes are very important, working with the windows to create the look of the whole design.

When your design has two or more colors, it is a good idea to use a stencil for each of your colors.

Simple stencil: The design of this stencil is to be used with only one color. For this reason, all of the design's shapes will be cut from the same stencil.

Multiple stencils: Repeating the same design, but this time using three different stencils, each corresponding to a color that will be used for the stenciling.

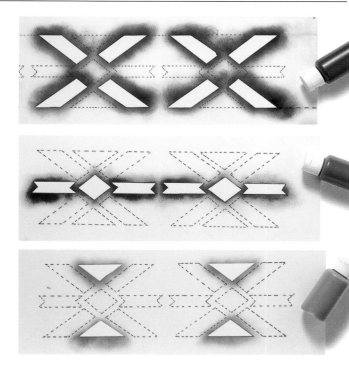

Registration marks

Most stencils have registration marks to perfectly align the image or design onto the surface to be stenciled. These marks are essential for the design to hold together visually and to line up, for instance, a frieze that runs parallel to floor or ceiling. In short, registration marks will keep your design from appearing crooked due to wrong positioning of your stencil.

There are various ways of making these registration marks, depending upon the type of paper used for the stencil. If the paper is translucent, as is acetate or polyester paper, the registration marks are generally indicated as broken lines. With opaque paper, such as manila paper, they are made with notches, cut into the edges of the stencil.

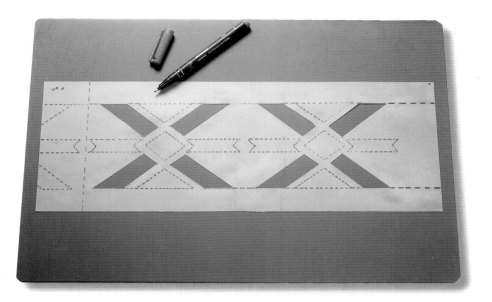

• Guidelines to align the design

Registration marks, drawn with straight, broken lines, are usually placed on either the upper or lower part of the stencil. They are used to place and secure the stencil in position for painting, lining it up correctly with your surface and with the rest of your design, for example, to situate a frieze design at a particular distance from the ceiling, or to place a border around the edges of a table.

• References for stenciling a repeated design

These are straight, broken lines that echo the outermost shapes of your design at its edges, and that are also placed at its beginning and/or its end. As you paint, the beginning of the stencil is placed in such a way that the broken line, the registration marks, serve to align the stencil exactly with the last configuration of stenciled shapes. An example of this would be a stenciled frieze that is continuous through a hallway or above a floor.

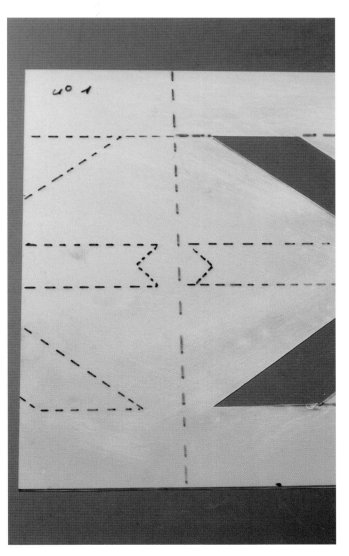

The broken lines that cross the bottom edge of this stencil serve as guidelines to place the design in the right position on the surface to be stenciled.

The fragment of the design, traced with broken lines at the left side of this stencil, serves as a reference point to maintain the same distance between each repetition of the motif. This prevents the frieze from becoming crooked.

• Controlling the different colors

This next series of broken lines, or registration marks, corresponds to each color in the design. The broken lines will mark out, on each stencil, the previously stenciled shapes. These marks are necessary to match up the second, third, and any other stencils with the area of design that has already been painted. For example, a red flower has to line up with its green leaves.

Each stencil corresponds to another. The broken lines that appear on stencil number two correspond to the shapes stenciled on number one. The shapes painted with stencil number two are indicated with broken lines on stencil number three.

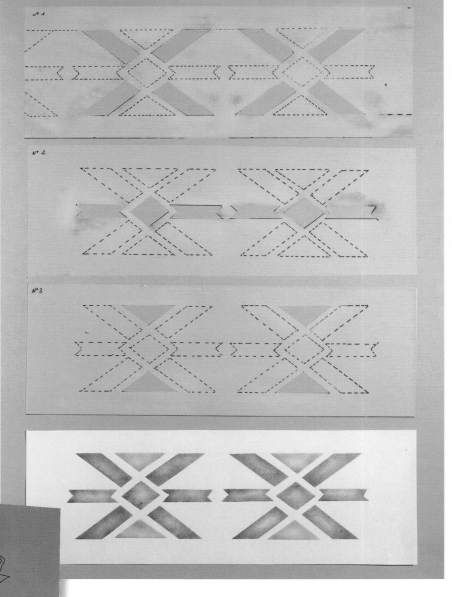

It is important that all the sheets of paper are cut the same size so that all the notches will match up. A sharp craft knife is a good tool to cut all the notches at the same time.

• Notches

Notches are especially used for opaque stencils, although they can also be used for polyester paper or other transparent stencils. Small notches or cuts are made at the edges of all the stencils that make up the design. In order to be able to do this accurately, all the stencils must be cut from sheets of material the same size. Before cutting out your shapes, separate pieces of paper are put together and are held in place with tape. Using a sharp craft knife, cut several V-shape notches in each stencil at the same time, at the top left or bottom right side.

Using a soft, sharp pencil, draw the notches of the first stencil onto the surface to be painted. Once you have painted through your first stencil, place the second one so that its notches line up with the notch marks of the first.

Composing a design for stenciling

Designing and composing a design for stenciling is easier than it sounds. In fact, you can do any kind of composition from the smallest image. It is important to take into consideration your experience and skill level before taking on a very ambitious project. Start simple, acquiring the skills you need as you work. Before long, you will be quite capable of tackling more and more complex projects. Stencil designs are versatile. One design can be adapted for many different compositions and an endless variety of surfaces, from walls to furniture, floors, fabric, and almost anything else you can imagine.

This fence is decorated with different individual elements placed randomly and spontaneously. These same elements used as a repeat on a table, for instance, would create a completely different composition.

Enclosed compositions in sequence

A sequential design runs along an area in a straight line, at regular and repeated intervals, and always in the same position. Its shapes are not isolated to make up another composition, and they are not meant to work by themselves; they are meant to work with unbroken symmetry.

Open compositions in sequence

An open sequence design runs across a space in a similar way as in the previous example, though now the shapes create composite or independent smaller designs. Their symmetry can be broken.

Friezes of fruit or flowers are a good example of open compositions used in sequence. The frieze can leave the straight linear composition by leaving spaces between each configuration of its bunches or groups of leaves and fruit, without the whole losing its harmony.

Isolated motifs that can be freely combined

Different motifs and shapes, such as plants, fruit, animals, and so on, taken separately, combined and recombined among themselves, can form a freestyle composition that is always changing and yet holds together. This composition is one of the most interesting and creative in stenciling. One of the perks of stenciling is that many of your stencils can be reused, combined in endlessly creative ways.

Enclosed combined motifs

These use enclosed central motifs that have strong individual impact. The shapes of an enclosed motif are part of a set of shapes that cannot be easily isolated for use in another composition, as they lose meaning. They seem nondescript by themselves. Sometimes they can be cleverly or creatively adapted for use in other projects by altering shapes and sizes for reuse.

This architectural frieze is a good example of an enclosed composition working in sequence. If the shapes are isolated, they have another impact entirely.

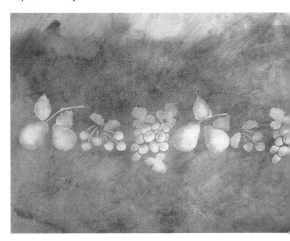

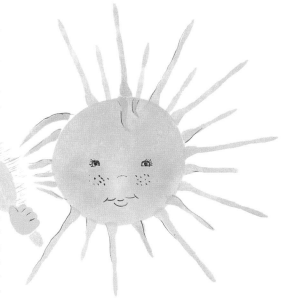

This sun is an enclosed combined motif as its shapes, if they are isolated, lose all their meaning.

Techniques for designing and cutting out a stencil

Designing and cutting out a stencil are slow and precise tasks. In this section we will discuss the steps of this process. We will begin by creating a stencil for a frieze inspired by a William Morris design. Next, we will create a design for a print. Before beginning your work, make sure that your work space has adequate lighting and that the table is protected with a cutting mat or a piece of glass for cutting your shapes.

Isolating and simplifying the design

When a chosen design consists of a multitude of elements, the first step is to choose the one that you consider to be most interesting and adapt it to the size you want by using a photocopier. Once the design has been isolated, it is necessary to simplify the drawing in order to adapt it to the stenciled image.

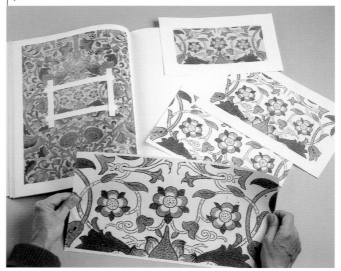

1- With tape, mark out and isolate the design of the print you are going to adapt for stenciling. Make photocopies of different-sized enlargements until you have the size you want.

2- Simplify the design as you trace it onto tracing paper and mark its bridges. In the example shown here, the shapes that are left seem too empty, so a floral figure has been added, selected from another part of the original design, to fill in.

3- On tracing paper, using different-colored pencils, mark the shapes you are going to reproduce.

Dividing the drawing into several stencils

If the design consists of several colors, you will want to make a stencil for each color. In order to do this you should have several sheets of your stencil paper ready. Here we are using polyester paper, each piece cut to the same size, one for each color. You will also need a permanent marker pen—the color is not important. In this exercise we have opted for a sequential, open composition that is suitable for use either as a frieze or as an isolated motif. It is very important to make guidelines and registration marks so that its alignment on your surface will be perfect.

3- Now, with a permanent marker pen of another color, trace your guidelines or registration marks. Once the design has been completely drawn, remove the masking tape and move the stencil to fasten it to your 3-inch (8-cm) space that has been reserved on the left side of your work (step 1). Draw the final fragments of shapes that will serve as a registration mark with straight, broken lines. Remove the stencil and replace it in its original position.

4- To make stencil number 2, place another sheet of polyester paper over the previous stencil. In this case it is not necessary to leave a margin of 3 inches on the left. Instead, reserve a 1-inch (2.5-cm) border on each side of the design. Number the stencil and label it with its color. Draw out the shapes that correspond to this color as with stencil number 1. When you have finished, trace your registration marks with broken lines, which will correspond to the registration marks for each of your colors. The broken lines should meet up exactly with the continuous lines drawn on the previous stencil, assuring that the painted design will properly align.

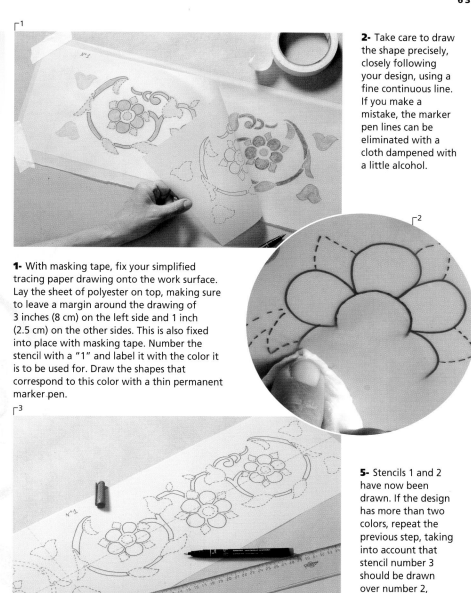

2- Take care to draw the shape precisely, closely following your design, using a fine continuous line. If you make a mistake, the marker pen lines can be eliminated with a cloth dampened with a little alcohol.

1- With masking tape, fix your simplified tracing paper drawing onto the work surface. Lay the sheet of polyester on top, making sure to leave a margin around the drawing of 3 inches (8 cm) on the left side and 1 inch (2.5 cm) on the other sides. This is also fixed into place with masking tape. Number the stencil with a "1" and label it with the color it is to be used for. Draw the shapes that correspond to this color with a thin permanent marker pen.

5- Stencils 1 and 2 have now been drawn. If the design has more than two colors, repeat the previous step, taking into account that stencil number 3 should be drawn over number 2, number 4 should be drawn over number 3, and so on.

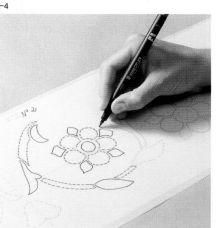

Cutting out a stencil

Before starting to cut out your stencil, it is a good idea to try out different cutting tools: a craft knife, an electric cutter, or small scissors. It is important to find the tool that you are most comfortable with and one that will cut precisely. Practice will give you the skills you need to use any of these tools. Do not forget that the stencil's shapes should be cut using continuous lines.

Using a craft knife

A craft knife can be used to cut most papers. It is important that the blade be kept sharp. If, while you are practicing with your polyester paper or acetate, the blade slips or needs too much pressure to cut with, it is time to change it.

1- Place the stencil on the cutting mat. Do not secure it in place. Hold the craft knife as if it were a pencil and place it firmly and vertically on the stencil, which you should hold in place with your free hand. Start to cut, pressing down on the cutting mat, always toward you, following the lines of the shape's edges. If the line is somewhat thick, make your cut at the outer edge.

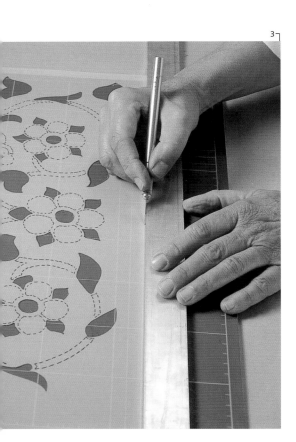

2- As you work, turn the stencil in the direction of your cutting, slowly, using your free hand so that you are always cutting toward yourself without raising the craft knife from the paper and cutting mat. This will help you maintain control and avoid making uneven cuts. Keep the cut-out pieces to make other stencils, or to flip-flop the design.

3- To cut out corners or parts that adjoin at an angle, two cuts are made that form a cross or an X shape. Straight lines should be cut out with the aid of a metal ruler, as the cutting tool will damage wood or plastic.

4- The second stencil should be cut out in the same way. Remember to cut out only the shapes marked with a continuous line.

Using an electric cutter

An electric cutter has a point as fine as a needle. It is used only with polyester paper or acetate as the cutting is done using heat, which would be dangerous to use with wood pulp paper. The needle point, once it is at the correct temperature, melts the polyester or acetate sheet. The point should not be touched when it is hot, and it should be left on a metal support between uses.

Place the stencil on a piece of smooth glass that must be larger than the actual stencil. The glass should be thick

enough so that it rests securely and does not slide on the worktable. The stencil is secured onto the glass with a spray mount or adhesive tape.

When the cutter heats to the correct temperature, hold the point in a vertical position on the surface of the stencil material and slowly cut out your shape with a continuous line, using very little pressure. Follow the instructions given on using a craft knife.

When cutting with an electric cutter, you should use a substantial piece of glass as a base. Secure the stencil to this and, when the cutter reaches the correct temperature, cut out slowly, following the lines of your shapes.

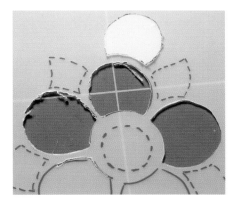

As an electric cutter melts the polyester paper, some rough edges may occur that can be rubbed or scraped away with your nail once all the design has been cut out.

With scissors

If cutting with a craft knife proves to be too clumsy, especially at first, scissors may prove to be a much better option. These should be small, very sharp, and fit comfortably in your hand; nail scissors or embroidery scissors are ideal.

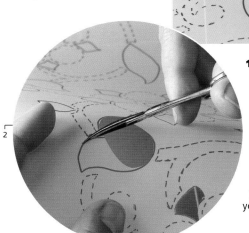

1- Hold the stencil in one hand and with the other make an incision with the point of the scissors at the top of one of the shapes.

2- Cut very carefully, following the outside lines of your shapes and moving the stencil with your free hand while you work.

How to transfer a drawing onto an opaque paper stencil

If you do not have polyester paper, use manila paper, pattern-making paper used by tailors and dressmakers, or cardboard saturated in linseed oil and left to dry. One advantage to using paper is that it can be cut out with greater ease and precision than plastic alternatives. The disadvantage of paper is its opacity. Making a stencil for designs that use many colors can present a major challenge, as paper cannot be washed and deteriorates quickly with handling; paper is a very good option for monochromatic designs and for stenciling with aerosol paint.

1. Once your design has been traced onto tracing paper, place some carbon paper between the manila paper and the tracing paper and fix both to your work surface. With a sharp pencil, go over the lines on the tracing paper again, checking from time to time to be sure the design is being correctly transferred.
2. Before cutting out your shapes, put all the stencils together and make the registration marks using the notch method (see page 60).
3. If the design is to be repeated many times, cut out several stencils of the same design to use in case the paper gets too damaged or breaks down with use.

To transfer the drawing onto the stencil, place carbon paper between the manila paper, which should be underneath, and the tracing paper, and go over the drawing with a very sharp pencil so that the lines are very clear.

How to correct mistakes

Cutting out a stencil requires a lot of patience, as it is easy to make mistakes, even if you have experience. For this reason, it is essential to think your work through carefully before you begin drawing and cutting.

One way to discover errors at a glance is to place your stencils one on top of the other and look at them in the light, checking that the cut-out shapes of the first stencil coincide with those of the second. However, the surest way to detect errors is to stencil the cut-out design onto a piece of paper. Sometimes, a small error may improve your design and it is not necessary for it to be corrected. Mistakes frequently occur with the windows and the bridges.

When the windows are very large, reconstruct the stenciling material with transparent tape, sticking it to both sides of the paper. Replace the stencil over the original design and draw the original shape again, cutting away the surplus tape with care. If, on the other hand, the window is very small, simply cut away the surplus paper to enlarge it. You can also use transparent tape to mend a bridge that has been mistakenly cut by sticking it on both sides of the stencil.

An easy way to look for possible mistakes is to put the stencils one on top of the other and hold them up to the light.

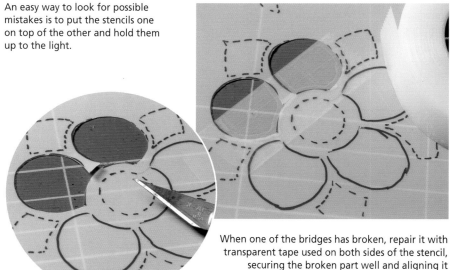

You can check for mistakes by stenciling the cut-out design onto paper and seeing how the design reads.

When one of the bridges has broken, repair it with transparent tape used on both sides of the stencil, securing the broken part well and aligning it properly. Then cut away the surplus tape.

Designing a printed pattern

One of the possibilities of stenciling is to imitate the pattern of fabric using a repeated shape or a simple design. A pattern is a design that is repeated at regular intervals, not necessarily equidistantly. These repeated motifs combine nicely with a frieze. The distance between your shape, or motif, depends on the area you need to cover and the size of the shape that you are going to repeat. Calculate the measurements of your surface before designing, considering the distance of shape placement and positioning relative to the rest of the pattern surrounding it. This process requires drawing some simple squares, though rhomboid shapes can also be used for diagonally placed repeats. The horizontal measurements will be different from the vertical ones for diagonally placed repeats.

4- Once all the hearts have been painted on the grid, place a similar-sized piece of polyester paper onto it and fix it in place. Draw the squares with broken lines, which will serve as guidelines and registration marks. Now draw over the hearts. Start with the heart at the center, using continuous lines, and then do the rest, alternating hearts drawn with broken lines with hearts drawn with continuous lines.

5- Cut out the hearts drawn with continuous lines.

1- For this project, choose a small motif. We have used a small heart shape. Draw the required size onto a piece of polyester paper and cut it out.

2- On polyester paper or mylar, rule squares at regular intervals. Do this by drawing a central vertical line from which you divide both sides into distances of about 3 inches (7 cm) and draw the vertical lines. Next, draw your horizontal lines at the same distance to make squares. These squares are necessary so that the intervals between the shapes are regular and the printed hearts are equidistant.

3- Place the heart stencil symmetrically over an intersection of squares and paint it. Now paint a heart at each intersection.

Printing repeat motifs in this way is an attractive way of complementing a frieze, for example for baseboards. From time to time and in a random way, you can stencil in a motif with another color, which will liven up the look of your pattern.

Tricks of the trade

Up to this point, we have discussed basic techniques for the adaptation of a design of several colors using corresponding stencils. However, there are other ways of accomplishing the same thing without having to cut out as many stencils. As you work, you are bound to discover your own tricks to save time and effort. Here are some we have discovered, and employ for their decorative usefulness and their simplicity. With only one stencil, we will make designs that, at first glance, seem to need more than one.

Proximity of colors

There are some multicolored designs for which it is not necessary to cut out a separate stencil for each color. Just be sure there is enough distance between shapes. This will depend on the width of the bridges between them. If they are more than an inch or so (2.5 cm), you can safely paint your shapes with different colors using only one stencil. This saves materials, work, and stenciling time since it won't be necessary to change the stencil with each color change.

Layering the shapes

It is possible to use only one stencil, shifting its positions to paint a design in several layers. The finished design is more complex than the stencil itself, which may be quite simple. The design motif is cut and used to decorate the surface. The stencil can then be repositioned and another layer of the design painted. This process can be repeated to build a complex design.

Following are several examples of layering shapes.

A flower

To stencil a flower in layers and repeated shapes, you need only design and cut out a stencil for one petal. The complete flower can then be stenciled by layering the shapes several times into a flower form, creating some beautiful transparencies.

This simple shape serves not only to stencil a beautiful flower, but it can also create a bouquet or border.

Shapes that are far enough apart to paint with different colors.

Checkered fabric

Draw a set of slanted lines of the same thickness at an equal distance from each other. Do another set below that one, but slanting in the opposite direction. Mark the guidelines and registration marks and cut out the stencil. Stencil in one direction with the cut-out shapes on the top part of the stencil. Line up your stencil and paint the crossing set of lines with the cut-out shapes on the bottom part. Keep your layer of paint light to create the transparencies so that the overlaps show.

Cord

You can stencil a cord design using a repeat as well, and also use only one stencil. This design can be used to frame another composition or to decorate small spaces.

First, design the shapes for the twisted fibers of a cord, leaving the same distance between each one. Then, cut them out alternately, skipping a shape in between. Now stencil a block of your design. Next, shift your stencil to the shapes that are blank, and paint again, completing the image of the cord.

Clouds and trees

Using only one round cut-out stencil shape, you can paint clouds, moving the stencil several times until you have achieved the desired form. Cloud masses are built with just this kind of repeated circular form. You can use the same process to paint the leafy round forms of a tree, using an oval stencil. Again, one stencil can be used to paint a row of trees to create a landscape in which each tree is different.

A gingham design is an attractive border to use in a child's room or in a kitchen.

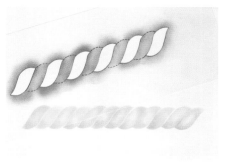

In this example, the cord has been stenciled in only one color. The design is also very pretty if you use two different colors.

Using one stencil, it is possible to create forms that have variety. The similarities and changing nuances create a charming look.

Grapes

Clusters and bunches of grapes can also be stenciled using this method. You need only cut out one grape and a few leaves. These simple stencil shapes can then be used to compose grape clusters of different sizes and an abundance of leaves. With only a couple of different-sized leaves you can stencil a very luxuriant grapevine, particularly if you use several colors of green.

As in the previous example, the richness of the design comes from the nuances in the repeated shapes.

An apple can be a pear

A stencil designed as an apple can be transformed into a pear by inverting the stencil. Stencil the apple in two different shades of red, the lighter one for the inner part and the darker one for the edges. The pear is stenciled with ocher with some light touches of green and red.

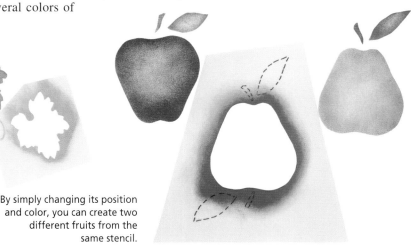

By simply changing its position and color, you can create two different fruits from the same stencil.

Economizing on stencils

In many cases it is not necessary to cut out a pile of stencils to do a large fruit or floral composition. Before starting to design and cut out the stencils for a design composition, it is important to think it through to simplify the task. With one or two cut-out shapes, you can obtain spectacular designs that are always different.

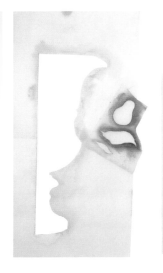

Half the urn has been cut out and stenciled. With one leaf and a pear you can go on to compose a complex cluster.

Flip the stencil of the urn over and stencil the other half. Use your stencils until you have reached the desired effect.

A Grecian urn with leaves and fruit

To stencil large objects such as urns, tubs, and containers, forms that are constructed of symmetrical right and left sides, you need only design a stencil that defines half of it. In our example we have used a Grecian urn. If a design of this complexity were cut out in its entirety, the results would have a more rigid look, without the richness of layering. To create this rich and beautiful design configuration, only a couple of leaves and a pear will need to be cut out. In this way you have the freedom to overlap and turn the direction of the stencil, building networks of shapes and layers of color. In addition, these stencils will always be useful for later compositions.

Stenciling over the edges

Up until this point, we have stenciled within the windows; however, by stenciling around the exterior edges of the cut-out shapes, you can get very unique results.

A frieze of leaves

Here's a design with large leaves. Cut your stencil and remove the positive shape to be used, rather than the window. Fix this piece to the surface and stencil very lightly around its outside edges. Move it to the middle of the unpainted area and repeat the previous step. Stencil up to the middle of each leaf so that the leaves appear to overlap.

With only one stencil shape of a leaf, you can create a very original leaf frieze.

Waves

To create waves, cut out a shape with a scalloped edge. Then, very lightly stencil the outside edge, making sure that the farthest edge is darkest. Shift the stencil down to change its position. Again, use your paint to stencil other waves, giving the effect of layers.

Waves. With one scallop-edged stencil you can paint a lively sea.

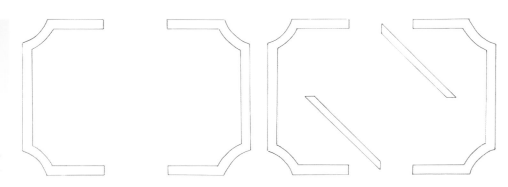

Combining two designs by using two stencils

Next, we will apply all the techniques previously described to a basically simple job that combines fruit shapes with geometric forms for its design. Begin the construction of the design using the shape of a square, a simple edging, and a centerpiece of some lemons and leaves. Though this is a simple, straightforward composition, it raises the usual problems. How can the fewest number of stencils be used to make up this design, being sure that all the shapes are gracefully joined with bridges, and how can the design be stenciled using three colors? We have solved the problem by strategically dividing the design into two stencils.

The first stencil. Draw the edge, leaving a separation, or bridge, of 3½ inches (10 cm) in the center. This bridge will secure the design structurally. Draw the corners of the square at the center of these bridges. The square, tilted on its axis, will contain the lemons in the middle of the design. Positioning the square, turned, in this way will serve to harmonize the two shapes.

Now we will concentrate on the square. It is impossible to include the whole of the perimeter on the same stencil, as the shapes would come apart. At the same time, some of the leaves overlap the edges of the shape on two of its sides. Here, the sides of the square that are not layered over by the leaves have been drawn.

The shapes of the lemons and the leaves will be painted with different colors, with their shapes very close together, so in this first stencil, we will draw only one of the two. For our example, we have decided to draw the leaves as they do not cut into the first two lines of the square that are already drawn.

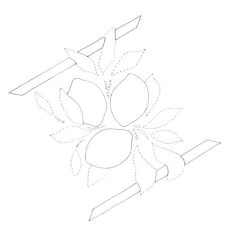

The second stencil. The lemons and the sides of the square that are cut by the leaves have been drawn onto this stencil. First, draw registration or positioning marks. Place the clean sheet of polyester paper on the first stencil and trace the leaves and the two sides of the square drawn on the first stencil, but using broken lines, making sure that they fit exactly. Then, draw the sides of the square that are cut by the leaves, and draw the lemons, using a continuous line.

chapter

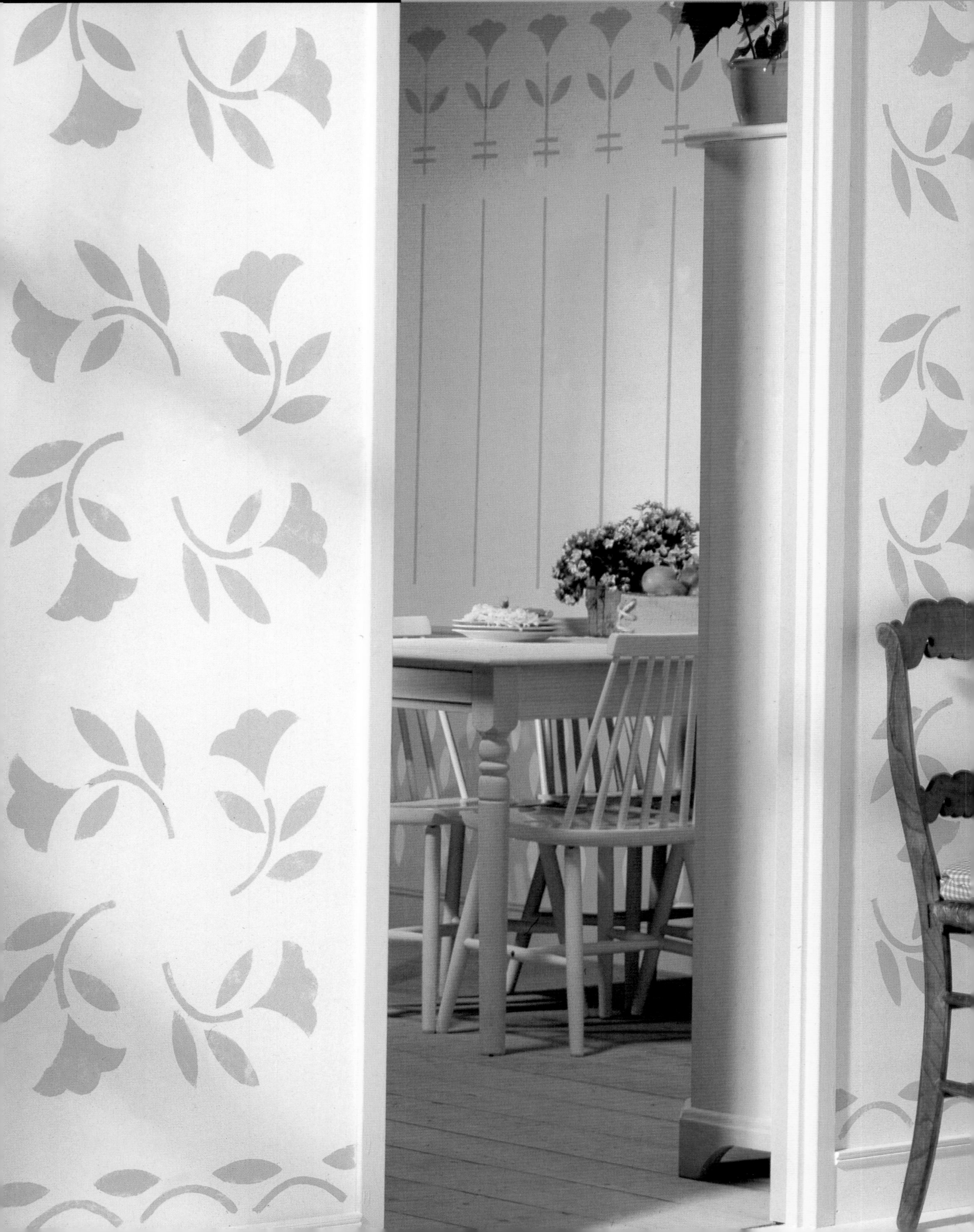

Stenciling on different surfaces

All the elements that go into the design of an area are important and need to make up a harmonious whole. Although stenciling is one of the most adaptable decorative arts for painting all kinds of surfaces, it is necessary to carefully assess the particulars of your project before starting. First of all, it is best to start by stenciling only one part of the room, using, say, a frieze or a border on one wall. Then you can decide if further stenciling of walls, fabrics, or other surfaces will improve or detract from the overall look. Stenciling is a decorative finish. If it is overdone, it can disturb the integrity of a room's decor, so it must be used with discretion. In this chapter we will explain how to prepare the various surfaces, how to plan their decoration, and how to stencil on them.

Stenciling on walls

Walls are the most basic design element when decorating a house. Their colors, textures, and patterns set the tone that will have a dominant influence on the whole. Beautiful furniture loses its impact placed against walls that don't support its charm and beauty. Stenciling is a beautiful, low-cost, doable way to handsomely embellish walls that will provide an elegant, warm, or lively feeling for the rest of a room's decoration. Stenciling affords great satisfaction that will last a long time.

A living room often contains furniture that is quite tall, such as bookshelves. One solution for equalizing their height to balance the rest of the room is to stencil friezes about 10 inches or so (25 to 30 cm) from the ceiling or, if the ceiling is very high, at about 3½ feet (1 m) from the floor. This can emphasize the style of the furniture and, at the same time, organize the space. If the area is quite empty, stenciling will add visual warmth while providing an original touch.

The corner of this children's room has been decorated by stenciling this frieze, which runs above the rocking chair about 10 inches or so (25 to 30 cm) from the floor.

Wall stenciling is so rich and decorative that it beautifully frames simple, functional furniture. Often, a home decorated with creative stenciling does not need a lot of furniture to be warm and welcoming.

Preparing the walls

Before beginning a stencil project, it is a good idea to evaluate the state of the walls to be stenciled so that the end result will be flawless. You will want to eliminate cracks, bumps, and dirt. However, you can also stencil with great success on old walls, as stenciling lends charm to some kinds of damage, emphasizing their antique look. An old surface should be painted with a matte plastic paint to prepare it properly, as satin gloss paint lacks the necessary porosity for the stencil to properly adhere.

Before starting your work, protect the floor with sheets of plastic or old newspaper, as some paint always drips and its removal can be problematic.

The best way to paint a wall is to use a felt roller and a large can of paint. The amount of paint you will need depends on the size of the wall, its color, and how many coats will be needed to cover it. Ask the people at your paint store for their expert advice.

It is advisable to protect light sockets and switches, as well as window frames, door frames, and any other surrounding structures, with masking tape.

Cracked walls

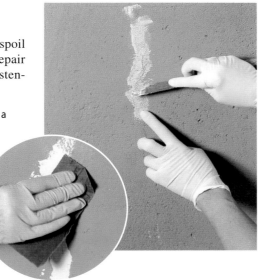

Walls that have cracks in them can spoil the stencil effect. It is better to repair them first before repainting and stenciling them.

Fill in the cracks using a spackle knife and a shrink-resistant spackle that you can buy at the hardware store, smoothing the surface until its imperfections are corrected.
When the spackle has dried, sand it down to eliminate any rough edges so that the filled surface is level with the wall. If the crack is very deep, repeat the process. Then paint the wall with matte plastic-based paint.

Smooth walls

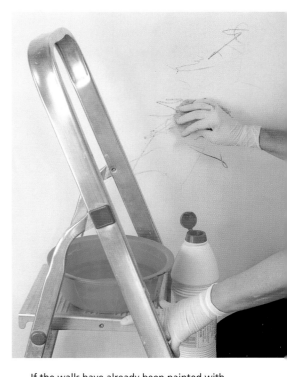

Smooth walls decrease the work of stenciling as they allow you to create transparent and finely blended shades. Edges will be precise and well defined; the stenciled color adheres well.

Distempered walls, walls painted with distemper, a mixture of pigment and sizing, cannot be cleaned and are not suitable for stenciling as the water and humidity of the acrylic paint will dissolve the distemper. In this case it is best to apply two or three coats of matte plastic-based paint over the distemper.

If the walls have been painted with satin gloss paint, it is advisable to repaint them using a matte plastic paint.

If the walls have already been painted with matte plastic paint but they are marked, they can be cleaned with warm water and some detergent. If they have been painted with plastic satin gloss paint, they should be repainted with two coats of matte plastic paint.

Textured walls

Although smooth walls are a wonderful surface for stenciling, they are not the only surface that takes stenciling well. Textured walls have a beauty all their own, giving wonderful effects when they are decorated. To do them well, you need to assess the nature and thickness of their texture.

In general, if the texture is thick or rough, a design consisting of small shapes would lose its definition and its effect would be lost.

Though this wall has a very rough finish, it still can be a receptive surface for stenciling. Textured surfaces have their own charm.

When stenciling on textured walls, it is best to use a design that has large shapes and a maximum of two or, perhaps, three colors.

Papered walls

In cases where wallpaper is in very bad repair, it is best to strip it off, replaster the wall, and prepare it, using two coats of matte plastic-based paint. If you do stencil over a wallpaper design that is too busy, say, to add any stenciling, glue down any parts that have come away from the wall and, after letting the glue dry for at least a day, you can cover it with a few coats of matte synthetic enamel paint (oil based) and then stencil over it using oil paints (see page 24). You should not paint with plastic paint, as the water content could dissolve the wallpaper's glue.

In some cases, as with wallpaper that is used to cover up cracks, or walls that are in a state of disrepair, removing the paper is not the best solution. Stenciling onto wallpaper can personalize a dull or outmoded paper. But if the wallpaper has some kind of pattern, you can, for instance, pull out the theme and further elaborate upon it.

How to organize your materials

Make your work space physically comfortable and productive. Unnecessary stopping and starting can be avoided if your materials are conveniently located within easy reach. The work of stenciling requires freedom of movement both of yourself and the stencil, as your work progresses along your surface. As surfaces may be large, the work is more tiring than just simply painting, so keep your materials organized and close at hand.

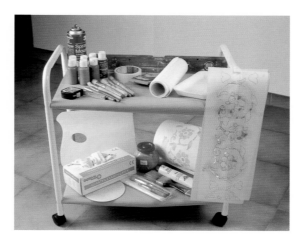

Organizing all your materials on a cart is one good solution when you are stenciling a large wall project, for example. As your work progresses, you can pull the cart along with you; your materials stay organized and handy at all times.

Here is a range of paint colors, gray-toned pastels, that work well for a multicolored stencil.

Base colors

Stenciling can be combined with practically any base color. However, for multicolored stencils and those with an aged look, a light-colored wall will set off the design. Light colors can range from off-white, grayish blue, grayish green, pink, and pale salmon to ochers and shades of orange. The color you choose will depend on the light in your room, furniture and its placement, and even whether your room is sparsely or densely furnished. If, on the other hand, you want to create a dramatic, contrasting effect, you can choose a dark background—navy blue, rust red, crimson, or English green, for example—and do a monochromatic stencil in white, gold, or some other lighter color. A tint of your base color can be very effective as a decoration on a dark wall.

The two top examples show a multicolored stencil design done on base colors of light ocher and pastel green. The two bottom designs are monochromatic stencils done on dark base colors. Notice the dramatic impact the dark backgrounds create. One is white on dark blue; the other is gold on rust red.

Friezes

Both horizontal and vertical friezes have many attractive application possibilities. The frieze has been used historically to decorate architectural spaces. It is useful for beautifully solving all kinds of spatial problems. Friezes tend to show off stenciling at its best. There is no other medium that can create continuity and repetition of design in such a uniform yet beautiful way. Although the space to be decorated may be very long, stencils make the work progress much more quickly than if it was done freehand.

Horizontal friezes

Horizontal friezes can be put either at the top of a wall, close to the ceiling, which serves to solve problems of excessive height, or they can be placed 3 or so feet (91 to 100 cm) from the floor to widen and organize an area. Friezes are very useful for framing an arch, a window, or a door, and for embellishing a flight of stairs.

On these pages we will show you different examples of how to apply horizontal stenciled friezes to decorate different areas of the house and to give some solutions to possible defects of space.

An entry hall is the first space encountered in the hall of an apartment house and therefore it sets the tone and conveys the design sense and personalities of the people who live there. In our example, the stenciling has been done on the landing of the second floor. The space is small, so the frieze has been placed at ceiling height to give the landing more height. The number corresponds to the apartment of the stencil artists. In this way, they have personalized this small space, distinguishing it from the other apartments in the building.

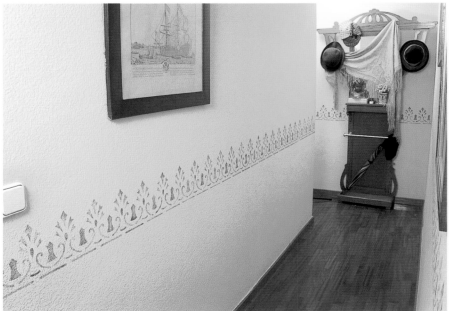

This narrow hallway is also very long and dark. The ocher base color and the stenciled frieze have not only widened it visually, but also shortened and cheered it up as well.

Frequently, the halls of present-day apartments are narrow, so you should look for solutions that will help to produce an optical effect of widening. In this hallway, a frieze has been stenciled to finish off the wall with stripes so that optically it will seem much wider than it actually is.

In this child's bedroom the frieze stenciled on the wall replaces the bed's headboard. Another possibility would be to stencil a frieze a few inches from the ceiling.

Before starting

Once you have decided which room and which area you are going to stencil, you will need to take stock of the room's size and characteristics. Stenciling walls takes careful preparation. You will particularly want to be certain that the size of the design adequately suits the room, particularly regarding friezes and borders. We suggest the following two starting points:

1. If you place the frieze at the top of the wall, you need to design its shapes so that the size of the overall decoration is big enough to read clearly and so that it visually suits the space and the character of the room's decor. If the room is very small, it is better not to plan too large a design with a lot of different colors, as it will tend to dominate the room.

2. The most practical thing to do is to make several photocopies of the required design, place them in the area you wish to decorate, and live with them for a few days. In this way, you will be able to confirm not only that you like the design, but also that the size and position are right.

In a kitchen it works well to place the frieze above the tiles if these do not reach the ceiling. If the wall cupboards also don't reach the ceiling, a frieze stenciled above them will finish them nicely. If there is a small dining area in the kitchen, run the frieze above it and on the upper part of the chair backs to differentiate the two areas. In the kitchen shown here, both the tiles and the furniture were gray. A Victorian frieze stenciled in bright colors, which runs entirely around the room and above the cupboards, has been painted to give the kitchen a warmer atmosphere.

A tip: Take time and plan; sockets and light switches should not cut into the middle of a border. However, with regard to doors and windows, it does not matter if a frieze that is about 10 inches (25 cm) from the floor is broken by one. If the frieze is placed near the ceiling, you should make sure that it runs above them and is a good distance from the lintel.

Stenciling a frieze with spaces in the design

This type of frieze is laid out in such a way that its placement along the walls is punctuated by a fixed space between one repetition and another. To plan a stencil of this kind, it is vital to carefully calculate the distance of these gaps between design motifs so that they fit the wall properly and the shapes are not broken or distorted by the corners. It is quite a common thing to discover that the floor and ceiling in an old house, as well as in even the most recent constructions, are not perfectly aligned. The solution for avoiding a crooked stencil is to use a level.

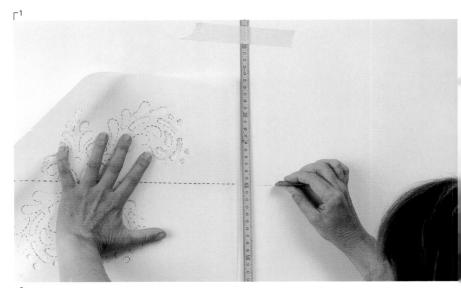

1- The first step consists of determining the height at which you are going to place the stencil. Measure this in relation to the floor and the ceiling and make a small mark with French chalk or a soft, sharp pencil (hard marks are very difficult to rub out afterward).

2- Draw a line that will indicate the position of the frieze's extension along the wall. Place the level horizontally so that it lines up with the mark made in the previous step. When the bubble is in the center, draw a line using small dots or a broken line that should be as faint as possible. Continue in this way, taking the next measurement from the marks already made until all the space has been covered.

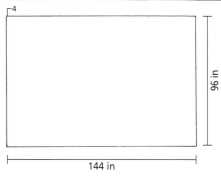

3- Calculate the size of each wall separately and from corner to corner; for example, 12 × 8 feet, or 144 × 96 inches. Once you have calculated the perimeters of the walls, measure the width of the design and calculate a logical distance between each repetition; for example: 12 inches + 2 inches + 12 inches + 2 inches, and so on.

96 in

144 in

4- Calculate how many times the design will be repeated along the wall. To do this, divide the measurement of the wall by that of the design. In this case: 144 ÷ 14 (design + space) = 10.28 and 96 ÷ 14 = 6.85. The design will be repeated 10.28 times on one side and 6.85 times on the other. It will therefore be necessary to adjust those .85 and .28 inch throughout all the length of the frieze. The easiest thing to do is to modify the spaces between the repetitions—the initial 1 inch—and divide them throughout the length of each wall. Don't worry if the distance between each design is different on each length of the wall. A difference of a fraction of an inch is indistinguishable. What is important is that the design maintains as similar a distance as possible between each motif on each wall and that it is not interrupted at the corners.

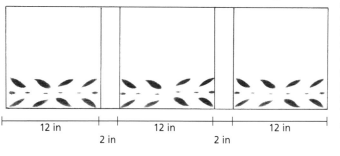

12 in   12 in   12 in

2 in   2 in

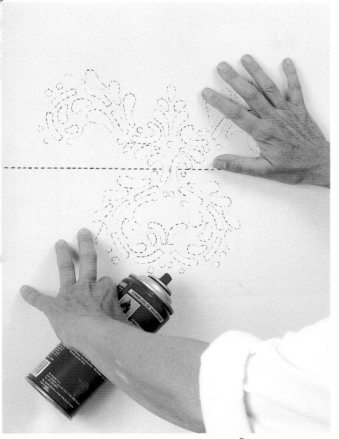

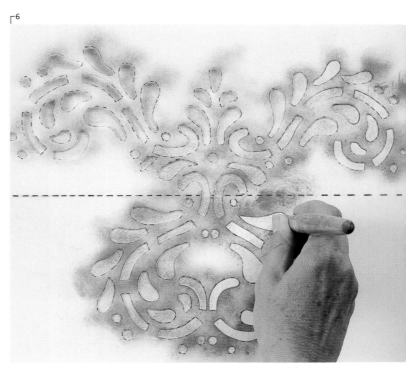

6- On the walls that have previously been prepared with matte plastic paint, you can stencil with any kind of paint using any method at all. In our example, we have used liquid acrylic paint and circular brushstrokes. Paint lightly, keeping the paint transparent. The disappearing edge will lend a slightly aged effect to your design, giving it charm.

5- Start to stencil in the area of your room that is least visible so that you can experiment with how the paint works. One good option is to start behind a door so that any mistakes will be hidden.

Place the stencil on the marks made on the wall with the French chalk and draw the horizontal registration marks with broken lines, which will help you to make sure that the design runs straight along the length of the space. Fix the stencil to the surface using a spray mount.

7- Once your design has been stenciled, lift up the stencil and shift it to the right, allowing for the distance between motifs previously decided on. Continue in this way until you have finished.

Stenciling friezes with continuous designs

Unlike friezes with spaces between the design, friezes with continuous designs do not need to depend on spacing and the isolation and repetition of their motif for their continuity. Instead, their look is fluid and constant as they run along their surface as a border. The most common examples of this kind of design are friezes that imitate architectural motifs, for instance, a vine with grapes or garlands of ivy. The great advantage of these is that you can start almost anywhere in your design as it doesn't depend as much on accuracy of measuring or consistent spacing. There is more leeway in a design like this, making easy compositions to stencil and a good exercise for the novice stencil artist.

1- Determine the height at which you are going to stencil your border.

2- Draw a guide line on the wall using a level. Then draw the horizontal guide lines and registration marks onto the stencil so that the design will be straight and the shapes will coincide at similar distances.

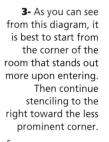

3- As you can see from this diagram, it is best to start from the corner of the room that stands out more upon entering. Then continue stenciling to the right toward the less prominent corner.

4- Secure the stencil to the surface and start painting, working to the right, starting from the prominent corner.

5- Now go back to the beginning and continue stenciling, moving to the left to finish off the corner that you have already stenciled.

6- Notice that this frieze, running the length of the wall, has fluidity and continuity.

How to stencil corners

As two walls meet at the corner of a room, so will your stenciling design, interrupting the continuity of the frieze.

In order to stencil the design so that its fluidity is uninterrupted, you will have to adjust the corners by eye, widening or narrowing the distance between the shapes and making sure that they are not bisected. Either one of two methods is useful here: Fold the stencil or cut it.

• Folding the stencil
Folding is the perfect solution if the stencil you are using is made of either medium thickness or thin polyester paper.

2- Once you have stenciled the first side, fix the other side of your stencil with adhesive tape, the side that in the previous step was left unfixed, and carefully lift up the first half of the stencil. Now, stencil in the same way, using smooth strokes.

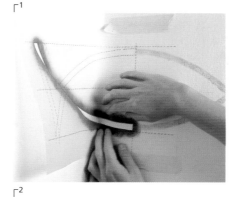

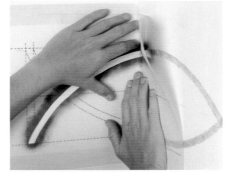

1- Fold the stencil against the wall in such a way that the design is flat, then fix it with adhesive tape on the side you are going to stencil first, leaving the other side unfixed. Stencil gently, using small dabs or by dragging the paint with a very dry brush, as you won't have much freedom of movement in this small space to stencil with circular movements.

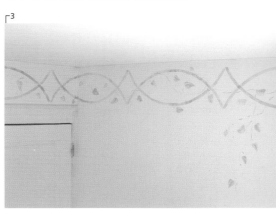

3- The corner is finished. It is unavoidable with such a continuous design that the horizontal flow will be somewhat disturbed, yet even this will work visually.

• Cutting the stencil
Cutting the stencil is used when the design of the frieze needs to look continuous. This is quite appropriate if you are working with manila paper or with thick polyester paper materials that are easily recut. It is practical here to cut out several duplicate stencils. If for various reasons this is not possible, stencil the frieze along the length of your wall, leaving the corners until last.

1- When you reach the corner, fold the stencil and mark out the place where it will be cut. With a craft knife or a pair of scissors, cut the stencil along this line.

2- Fix the cut stencil in the corresponding place and protect the other side with thick paper or cardboard. Stencil with the stipple method, using gentle strokes.

3- Remove the stencil from the painted side and fix the other part of the cut stencil to the adjoining wall. Protect the side you have just stenciled with cardboard, then paint.

4- The finished stencil.

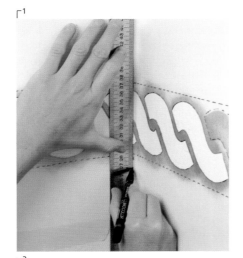

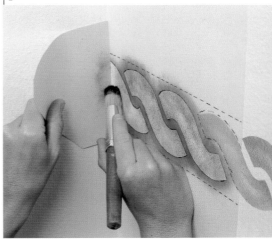

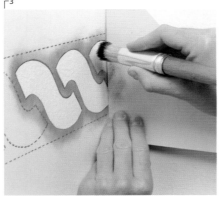

Vertical friezes

Stenciling a vertical frieze will give your wall decoration a particularly original look. To stencil a vertical frieze effectively, first take into account the vertical position of the wall and assess its irregularities. As with a horizontal frieze, the first task consists of drawing accurate lines. To draw a true vertical onto your wall, you can drop a plumb line or, of course, you can use a level.

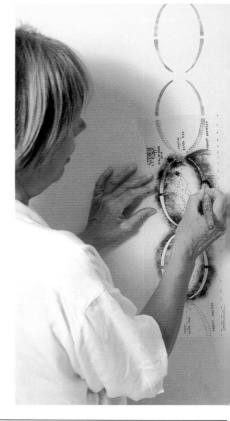

Here is the first step, drawing a vertical line onto your wall with the aid of a level. When doing a vertical stencil, you can guarantee that the frieze runs vertically by drawing and following the guide lines on both the wall and the stencil, which must coincide.

Stenciling friezes vertically can be an original design solution for decorating a wall. This kind of decoration is particularly suitable for rooms with very low ceilings.

Framing doors and windows with friezes

Stenciling a frieze can attractively enhance architectural elements such as doors and windows. There are no limits to the sort of motifs that will work well, from faux stone architectural compositions, to very symmetrical cords, to open lyrical compositions that meander freely, even breaking the straight line of the design's corners. Unless you choose the last option, the most common problem is how to solve the angle or the point where a horizontal and vertical frieze meet. Before starting, you should analyze the different possibilities. It is very useful at this point to do various frieze designs and place them on a table, forming one or two angles, similar to the way you would place them on the object you are going to frame. You can proceed in several ways:

1. Design a new element or motif that complements the angle; one way to approach this is to analyze the composition of the shapes so that you can do a drawing relating to them.

2. Adapt some of the shapes of the design; in the case of designs with soft, curved, fluid shapes, it is fairly simple to adapt one of the shapes for the corner so that the flow is not interrupted. To do this, isolate one motif or section and make another stencil that visually extends beyond both the vertical and horizontal lines of the frieze.

3. Another option for the corner is dividing the design diagonally at the point where the horizontals and verticals meet. Draw a diagonal line from the interior angle to the exterior one, forming a dovetail. This will make it unnecessary to cut a new stencil.

4. Continue with the horizontal frieze until the end. The vertical frieze is simply placed at right angles to the horizontal design, continuing to construct its frame. The corners where the friezes coincide are the most complex aspect of a frame frieze. Check where they should be cut and where and how the two friezes should meet.

The frieze that frames this door has been used to enhance it.

The frieze that finishes off and frames these shelves gives continuity to the wall and makes the space seem larger.

Doing panels

On many occasions, the combination of vertical and horizontal friezes can be used to divide a large wall into panels, breaking up its surface to obtain a new, warmer structure that loses some of its formality. Panels are a good decorative solution for walls or narrow hallways that have no doors and into which no other decorative element will fit. They are also suitable for areas decorated in a classic style and are perfect to highlight collections of porcelain, antique engravings, prints, or paintings.

The best way to plan decorative panels is to draw a scale plan of the wall and try out different compositions. You can even do different combinations of panels of the same or different sizes. It can be very attractive to use an uneven number of panels, even of different sizes, as the central panel will then be a pleasant focus.

To calculate the size of the friezes that will make up the panels, follow the instructions given previously for stenciling friezes that have spaces between the motifs, and friezes with continuous designs (see pages 80–83). It is especially important to follow the instructions for corners (see page 83) and to use a plumb line and a level so that the design coincides perfectly horizontally and vertically. Stencil the horizontal friezes and then the vertical ones.

Do all the planning before decorating a wall with panels.

It is very useful to draw a sketch to scale to be able to plan everything. Breaking the design of the wall into an uneven number of panels can be an attractive solution.

Use a level and a plumb line to find accurate horizontal and vertical positions for the friezes.

Once the two horizontal friezes have been stenciled, stencil the verticals. Here, we have also started from the center.

Start by stenciling the horizontal friezes. Here, because of the nature of this design, we start the stencil in the middle, so that the four facing leaves coincide at exactly the right point.

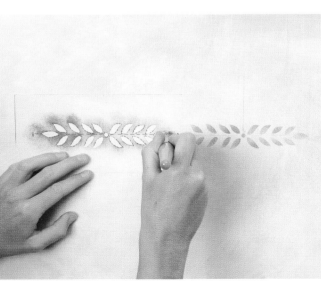

Combining individual motifs

Individual motifs can be compositions of quite a considerable size, playing a dominant visual role in the decoration of a wall. Sometimes, taking several separate individual motifs and stenciling them in combination can create a beautiful result. They can be the central design for walls that have been paneled with either small friezes or moldings of stenciled cords. A large design of combined motifs can work well in irregularly shaped places. They can serve to tell a story on the walls of a child's bedroom, while working as a charming decoration.

This orange tree is a perfect example of a combined individual motif that functions in a central visual role. Using stencils of leaves, one of oranges, one for the trunk, and another for a large earthenware jar, we have created a harmonious picture.

Here, the design has been centered in a panel. The first step is to draw the central vertical line of the panel, then locate its center point. In addition, locate the center of your design. Center this stencil on your wall panel and assess the effect. Here, the top of the tree bears so much of the weight of this composition that we have left a little more space at the top to balance it.

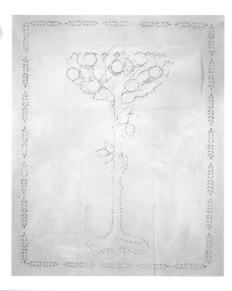

Centralized individual motifs

These are the dominant motifs of a design that play a primary visual role, and that are placed in the center of a panel, a stretch of a wall, or on a door. It can be very attractive to stencil these lightly, or even sand them down, or stencil them onto an aged-looking wall, in the style of antique frescoes or murals. Before starting, make several different-sized photocopies of your chosen design and decide which would be the most suitable for the area you wish to decorate.

Off-center individual motifs

Here, we are randomly combining several isolated motifs or closed combined motifs to form another composition that is more complex or that tells a tale, for example, stenciling a short story in a child's bedroom by using a series of different motifs (animals, toys, cars, and so on). Another idea is to stencil a whole wall from floor to ceiling, using a wide variety of shapes or only a few.

This child's bedroom is a delightful example of the placement of a thematic motif that uses a combination of stencils that have been freely positioned to tell a story about gnomes. Even the playhouse has been incorporated into the story by decorating its surfaces with stenciled designs.

A composition with individual motifs

When planning a stenciled children's story, place it at a suitable height so that it can be seen by the child, making sure that the pictures are not covered up by the furniture.

1- It is a good idea to assess the sizes of the different motifs that will make up the story. For example, if you are going to stencil a story that includes several animals, toys, trees, and other elements, you will want the relationship between their sizes to be as realistic as possible, so that trees, for instance, are bigger than the animals, and so on. It generally works better visually to make up your composition using a few large elements rather than a lot of small ones, so that the story is told clearly and the images are not too busy and confusing, particularly for a child.

2- Work toward a balanced composition by placing the photocopied designs in the positions that look best. Here, they have been placed next to each other, to tell the story in a linear way. By using photocopies, lining them up in story order, you will be able to judge the way the sizes relate to each other and make any necessary changes at this stage.

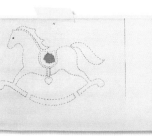

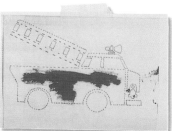

3- Once you have decided on the composition of the storytelling motifs, design a border for a finished look. This could be either a simple frieze, a vine, or a faux molding. We have used a simple border frieze. After determining the height of your decorations, draw the registration marks and stencil the border frieze first. Notice the way this gingham border supports the general composition.

4- First stencil the bigger motifs. Place the motifs by eye in relation to the frieze. Instead of doing a lot of measuring, and to avoid having to draw a second horizontal guide line on the wall, draw a pencil line on the paper, marking the distance between the placement of the first motif and the frieze. This mark will serve as a guide to placing the following motifs at the same height.

5- Now stencil in the smaller elements. These should serve to reinforce or support the larger elements. If you choose to, you can finish off the composition with the same frieze, or even with a different one, to border the upper part of the design, which will give it a more compact appearance.

Prints

A print is a design made of shapes that are repeated to cover a particular area, maintaining consistent distances between shapes. The repeat of the shapes in this way makes an ordered, uniform design.

There are a multitude of applications for print-type designs. They can be used to enhance the walls of a room, giving the illusion of fabric or wallpaper, or they can continue a wallpaper print onto baseboards, and so on. The difference between stenciling a print and covering the wall with fabric or wallpaper lies in the creative possibilities stenciling offers. For example, stenciling gives you the freedom to introduce different shapes from time to time, and it allows you to modify the colors as well. In short, it allows you to add a touch of originality to your design by introducing unique elements to an otherwise very regimented composition.

Bedrooms, children's rooms, and hallways are the perfect places to use a stenciled print. Prints that imitate damasks in the interior of a panel are also very attractive.

To do a regular print, which will evenly cover your designated area, you will have to think through the particulars and design your pattern carefully. Bear in mind that walls are usually irregular, even if they don't appear to be. Be sure to take your measurements carefully as there are bound to be variations.

A stenciled print has the charm of a hand-made print since, despite being a composition that is as organized as a wallpaper or fabric pattern, each one of its shapes is painted with varying intensities of color.

1- After making up the stencil with the design you wish to use (see page 76), draw a vertical broken line in the middle of your wall with French chalk or a soft pencil. Should you wish to stencil a dado rail, a design that decorates the lower part of your wall, it is usual for its top edge to be placed at about 3 feet (90 cm) from the floor.

2- Place the stencil at the highest point of your vertical line, positioning it in such a way that its central shape, drawn at its intersecting grid lines (indicated with a broken line), coincides with the vertical line you have drawn on the wall.

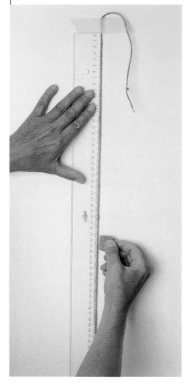

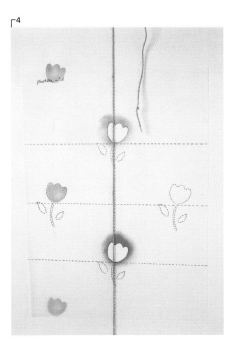

3- First paint the cut-out shapes of your design. Now lift up the stencil, shift it farther down the wall, and line up the shape used for positioning (drawn onto the stencil with broken lines) with the last stenciled shape. Continue stenciling vertically until you reach the floor, always making sure that the line on the stencil coincides with the vertical line you drew on the wall.

4- Once the central area of shapes has been stenciled, continue the process with the right-hand area. Place the stencil in such a way that the shapes drawn with the broken line at the left margin of the stencil coincide with your painted shapes. Repeat the stenciling process from top to bottom until you again reach the floor. It is important to keep checking, using a plumb line, that the stencil lines up vertically. Even small deviations can throw off the clean look of your pattern.

5- When the right-hand portion of the wall is finished, return to the central area and place the stencil in such a way that the positioning lines drawn at the right of it coincide with the shapes stenciled on the central line of the wall. Now stencil in the left-hand area of your design.

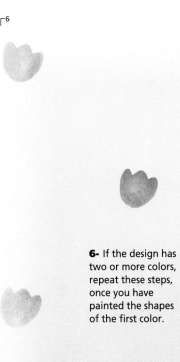

6- If the design has two or more colors, repeat these steps, once you have painted the shapes of the first color.

Tricks of the trade

No two people develop their skills at the same speed. In the same way, you can be sure that everybody, once they know what decorating with stencils is all about, will go on developing their own methods and tricks to solve small but persistent problems.

Errors of planning and other problems such as ripping up the surface of the paint with the tape, or making a mistake with the size of the design, are some common experiences you can have while you are learning. The following are some of the tricks of the trade to help you avoid the most common of these problems.

Before designing or cutting your stencil, experiment with different sizes. You can do this by using photocopies, or by stenciling your design onto a piece of cardboard and doing some tests with different colors.

Tape your test pieces onto the wall, in possible stencil places, and live with them for a few days to see which work best for you.

Be sure to save enough of the paint that you have used for your design. This can be used to correct small mistakes or for touch-ups later, rather than having to match the color and remix. Use glass jars and label them clearly, indicating which areas you have painted with each color.

Try to make sure that the adhesive tape does not stay on the wall longer than necessary. When you remove it, it is easy to also remove some of the paint from the wall. This is all too common, particularly when dealing with walls that are not well sealed, or if their plaster base has deteriorated. To lessen the strong adhesive bond of your tape, you can first stick it onto a piece of fabric. Your clothing will do, and the tape is now less likely to damage your painted surface.

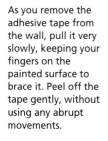

As you remove the adhesive tape from the wall, pull it very slowly, keeping your fingers on the painted surface to brace it. Peel off the tape gently, without using any abrupt movements.

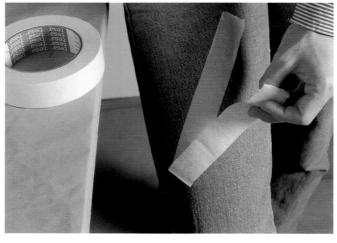

When a design has two or more colors, first paint all the shapes of one color, then follow with the next color.

Correcting mistakes

Don't be discouraged if at first you make mistakes, even if you have carefully thought your project through. All kinds of situations can arise as you work that cannot be foreseen until you have acquired a certain amount of experience.

At the same time, you need not feel too anxious about making mistakes because there are many ways of correcting them. Even if, once the surface has been stenciled, the work is not satisfactory, you can always paint over sections of it, or even start over again from the beginning.

Some mistakes are practically invisible on a large surface, and can even give the work a certain charm, the look of the unique irregularities of work painted by hand. Stenciling is not a mechanical process but a work of handcraftsmanship.

3- Plastic-based paints dry more or less quickly, depending on the temperature of the room, atmosphere, and weather. To speed up the drying process you can use a hand-held hair dryer. Once the paint surface is completely dry, you can fix the stencil in place and start stenciling again.

1- Paint can be taken off a surface by sanding or by cleaning it with warm water and a scouring pad before it has been allowed to dry too long. If you have used acrylic paint, we recommend doing this within 24 hours.

2- Once the paint has been removed, apply two coats of the paint you have reserved.

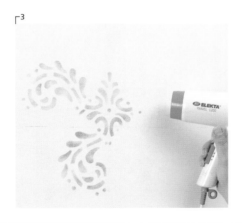

4- Use an eraser to lighten designs that are too dark.

Adding the look of aging

Adding the look of aging to a wall or stenciled design can be uniquely charming for a country house, for example, or wherever that look may enhance a space. Sandpaper, scouring pads, and washes of different colors are the things you will need to imitate the passing of time.

This frieze has been stenciled with a patina of gray that gives it a strong contrast with the white background.

1- When the paint is dry, sand it very lightly so that the shapes will become an integral part of the wall, giving the appearance that it has been there for years.

2- Once it has been sanded, apply either a darker or lighter wash, depending on the degree of aging you wish to achieve. Here, we have used a burnt umber, which gives a very subtle look.

Stenciling on wood

Traditionally, decorating furniture has depended on the quality of the wood it is made of. Woods such as mahogany, walnut, rosewood, teak, and maple really need no decoration, as the wood has its own beauty. But plain woods such as pine, or old and painted furniture, can be antiqued, updated, or simply adapted to a new environment. Stenciling on wood requires rigorous preparation of the surface as well as a final coat of varnish to enhance and protect the work.

This chest of drawers was found next to a garbage can. Stenciling transformed it into the focal point of a room.

The details painted on these cut-outs of bears have been done with stencils.

The stenciling on the top of this aged table has greatly increased its charm.

Preparing the surface

The wood surface to be stenciled should be porous, and free of dust, silicone residues, and grease. It should be cleaned and sanded until it is smooth to the touch.

The preparation of the surface will vary according to the condition of the wood: whether it is old or new, whether it is untreated or has been previously painted or varnished.

Raw or clean wood

This is wood that has not been painted, varnished, or waxed, and that we want to stencil and leave the grain of the wood visible.

It is very simple to prepare this type of surface. It will be necessary to first sand it thoroughly in order to leave the surface free of dust and dirt, and smooth and even.

Before stenciling the surface, in some cases it is a nice idea to apply a dye or stain to change the tone or color of the wood without hiding the grain. It is generally better to apply several coats of a light-colored stain than to use a deeper color. If an oil-based stain is used, it will not soak into the wood fibers, so it is not necessary to sand the surface again. But if a water-based stain is applied, it is quite likely that the surface will appear rough again because water-based stains and dyes tend to raise the woody grain. In that case, the surface must be sanded smooth again and cleaned to remove all traces of dust before stenciling.

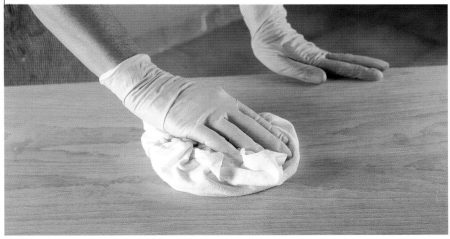

1- Sand the surface in the direction of the grain, with grade 0 sandpaper first and then 00, until it is perfectly smooth. Wrap the sandpaper around a sponge or a block of wood to exert uniform pressure and to increase leverage.

2- Remove all traces of dust with a cloth or a vacuum cleaner.

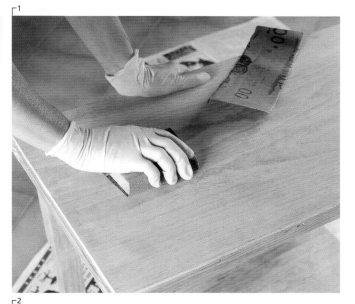

3- Shake the bottle of dye or stain well and apply, using a wide brush in parallel strokes and following the direction of the grain. Before it is completely dry, stroke the brush over the surface repeatedly to spread the color evenly. Apply additional coats until the required depth of color is achieved. Allow it to dry completely. In this case, a wood dye has been applied that does not soak into the wood fibers and therefore does not require sanding again.

Painted wood in poor condition

With wood surfaces or furniture that has been previously painted or varnished and badly damaged, or if you simply want to change the color, the first step is to remove all traces of paint or varnish. Although this can be done with sandpaper or a solvent, it is more effective to use a chemical paint and varnish stripper. Protect your hands with thick rubber gloves and wear a mask, as this stripper is highly toxic.

3- Place the removed paint on a piece of newspaper. Protect other surfaces, as the stripper is highly corrosive.

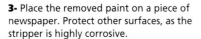

1- Apply a generous coat of stripper with a wide brush, completely covering the piece of furniture. Leave for 10 to 15 minutes until the paint cracks ("crackles"). Follow the manufacturer's instructions regarding the time needed for the paint or varnish to soften.

2- After the paint or varnish crackles, remove the mixture of paint and stripper, using a steel stripping knife for the flat surfaces. For rounded legs or columns, use grade 0 steel wool. Repeat the process until all the paint or varnish has been completely removed.

4- Rub the clean surface with grade 0 steel wool soaked in turpentine or paint thinner to remove any chemical stripper left on moldings, carvings, or in any crevices. Do this very carefully, as any stripper that remains could mar the coat of paint or varnish applied subsequently.

5- Before the piece of furniture is completely dry, clean off any traces of dirt with a cloth soaked in turpentine.

Painted wood in good condition

If the piece of furniture is already painted with matte plastic-based paint that is in good condition, it is only important to clean off any dirt and traces of silicone that furniture polishes tend to leave behind. To do this, use a cloth soaked in soapy water or turpentine. Try not to wet the furniture too much, as the water can dissolve the glue of veneers, and of legs, moldings, and other parts. You can use the same method to prepare furniture that has been varnished or painted with gloss paint that is in good condition.

On varnished or painted furniture in good condition, simply clean the surface with a cloth soaked in soapy water or turpentine.

Stenciling on raw or clean wood

Once the surface has been properly prepared, and before starting to paint, study the piece of furniture to decide which patterns will look attractive, as well as where to place them. Be sure to measure the piece so that you can adapt the pattern or patterns to the parts you wish to decorate.

The most suitable paints for stenciling on clean wood are liquid acrylics or acrylic creams. Paint with circular strokes, using a light touch to maintain transparency so that the wood grain can still be seen.

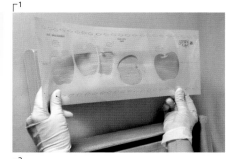

1- Chalk a 90-degree cross in the middle of the stencil to mark the center of your chosen design. Now mark the center of the tabletop using the same method and line up the stencil with the tabletop so that the centers of the crosses coincide. Anchor the stencil to the surface.

2- Using white acrylic paint and circular brushstrokes, stencil your design onto the tabletop. The shadows are painted in yellow acrylic paint.

3- Once you have finished the tabletop, paint the legs.

4- When the paint is completely dry, varnish over it with a soft, clean brush, following the direction of the wood grain.

Stenciling on plastic paint

The great advantage of stenciling furniture using plastic-based paints is that they are extremely fast-drying, allowing you to paint several coats in a matter of hours. As plastic paints are often used to paint walls, the same paint can be used for walls and furniture to coordinate a whole room. Plastic-based paints are not as resilient as oil-based paints, so they should be used on pieces that will not get much wear and tear. You can start with furniture that is already painted the desired color, or use plain wood pieces that you can paint with two or three coats of matte plastic paint.

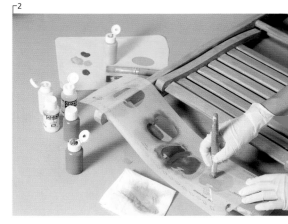

1- Fit and anchor the stencil over the area you wish to decorate, in this example, a wooden folding chair.

2- Stencil with acrylic paints, using the traditional method of circular movements.

3- A matte acrylic varnish has been used to protect the blue-painted finish of the chair. Acrylic varnish will not yellow.

Stenciling on varnish or gloss paint

It is a good idea for furniture that is used frequently and gets a lot of wear and tear to be covered in varnish or gloss paint, as this finish will last longer. Oil-based varnish and high-gloss paints give a smooth, shiny, unporous finish. Before stenciling, the surface must be completely clean and dry. The best paints to use for stenciling onto oil-based finishes are oil paints in tubes, sticks, or jars. Use the stippling method to paint, which will allow you to create a flat tone, mixing the oil paint with a little varnish as you work to reduce drying time and create some transparency.

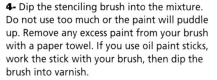

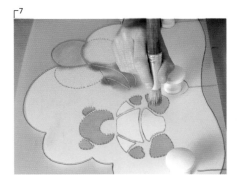

1- Once you have chosen your design and determined its composition and color, put your oil colors on a palette and pour a small amount of varnish into a receptacle.

2- This stencil has been cut to fit around the pegs of a clothes hanger. The stencil is then anchored to the surface.

3- With a small brush, mix just a little varnish with each of your oil colors.

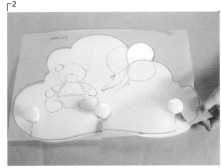

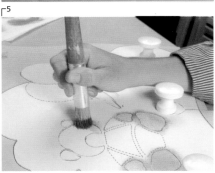

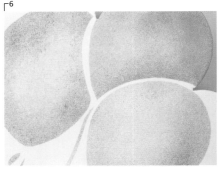

4- Dip the stenciling brush into the mixture. Do not use too much or the paint will puddle up. Remove any excess paint from your brush with a paper towel. If you use oil paint sticks, work the stick with your brush, then dip the brush into varnish.

7- Wait half an hour before doing the next stencil so that the colors already painted are dry and not tacky, and won't stick to the stencil when it is placed on top.

8- Wait a good 48 hours to allow the stencil to completely dry, then paint it with a coat of varnish. Do this by replacing your cut-out stencil over the stencil-painted area, and dab gently with a stencil brush dipped in a small amount of synthetic varnish.

5- Stenciling the bear: Holding the brush at right angles to the surface, stipple the paint on by tapping lightly, working inward from the edges.

6- Without waiting for the paint to dry, layer the color around the edges to create shadows, in the same color or using a darker shade. In this way, the paint layers work like glazes, creating gentle gradations.

Imitation wood inlay

Marquetry, or wood inlay, consists of forming decorative patterns by inlaying woods of different colors and qualities. Inlay is a mark of high-quality furniture making, but the look of inlay can be created with stenciling and is suitable for all types of furniture, wooden boxes, and other objects. Choose paint colors that most closely resemble wood tones, such as burnt umber, burnt sienna, ivory, or black. You may want to design a motif that picks up on the style of the piece of furniture you are working with, though it is always a good idea to use the traditional geometric forms often used in marquetry. Follow your stenciling with a coat of varnish. A simple piece of furniture can be transformed into a work of art using stenciling to simulate inlay's beautiful look.

1- Begin stenciling using a base color, creating the desired shades. On unvarnished wood such as this raw wood file box, use liquid acrylic paints.

2- Traditional inlay patterns are geometric in character. This composition has been designed as a grid. The colors used resemble the tones of different types of wood.

3- To paint the circular design that is made up of eight pie-shaped pieces, cut four of them in a circle that will be shifted to paint the second four. The other geometric designs in two colors can be handled using the same method. The stencil is anchored, and paint is applied in a light mahogany color.

5- Stencil the other geometric shapes the same way, combining different wood colors.

4- Now turn the stencil 45 degrees, until the cut-out shapes fit perfectly between those already stenciled. Anchor the stencil again and paint in a dark mahogany.

7- Once all the geometric shapes have been stenciled, apply varnish following the direction of the wood grain.

6- To imitate thin strips of inlaid ebony, you can highlight the shapes by finishing off the edges freehand using fine strokes in black. The same can be done with white to imitate ivory.

How to protect your work with varnish

Knowing how to give a stenciled surface a beautiful finish is important for its look and for its durability. A good finish not only guarantees lasting protection, but also enhances the overall look of the piece.

The best finishes for stenciled wood surfaces are varnish and wax. Varnish creates a finish that is lasting, protecting the piece from the wear and tear of constant use. It also gives the surface a luminous quality, emphasizing and deepening the colors.

Once the piece has been varnished, you can also use mediums to create patinas with an aged look, create crackling, or simply apply a good wax.

Varnishing

Traditional, synthetic, or acrylic varnishes can be used. Varnishing is a simple procedure but it must be done with care and the varnish given plenty of time to dry. Varnishing should be followed with fine sanding to give it a smooth, satiny finish.

1- Using a clean brush, apply the first coat of varnish diluted with 10 percent solvent. Work first in the direction of the grain, which will extend the varnish, giving it an even coat that completely covers the surface. Next, work in the direction opposite to the grain, using a light touch so the brushstrokes are invisible. Leave to dry completely, then apply a second coat, this time with the varnish undiluted.

2- When the surface is completely dry, before applying the third coat, sand gently with water-dampened sandpaper, fine grade 240, and then 360. Clean away the dust and apply the third coat. Allow to dry completely.

Patinas to age the wood finish

The aging effect gives furniture a beautiful warmth. To achieve this, a dark patina must be applied to the varnished piece. If you want to further increase the aged look, you can mar, or finely coarsen, the stenciled surface before varnishing by rubbing it very gently with grade 000 steel wool so that the raw wood shows through in some areas. Then varnish, leave to dry, and apply the dark patina.

1- After varnishing, apply the dark patina with a brush. This patina will imitate the look of the dirt and residues that accumulate on furniture with time.

2- Use a cloth to remove some of the patina before it dries. An aged effect is more attractive if it is subtly crafted.

Crackling

This effect imitates varnish that has cracked due to changes in temperature. Once the effect is achieved, a patina is applied so that the cracks in the varnish are emphasized by its darker color. Crackling is achieved by applying a quick-drying varnish on top of a slow-drying one. The first pulls at the second, causing cracks to form.

In craft stores, hobby shops, or even hardware stores, you can find various crackling media that are easy to use, both water and oil based. Simply follow the manufacturer's instructions.

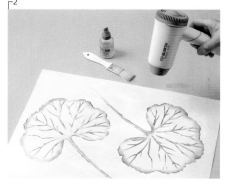

1- Homemade crackling: Apply a generous coat of undiluted latex or vinyl resin (slow-drying varnish) onto the stenciled surface. Allow to dry until it is tacky without sticking to the fingers.

2- Now apply a second coat of varnish, this time quick-drying gum arabic, again spreading it uniformly with a brush. Leave it to dry. Cracks will soon appear. You can speed up the drying/crackling process with a hair dryer, held about 8 to 10 inches (20 to 25 cm) from the surface of your piece, so that it doesn't burn.

3- Once the desired effect is achieved, apply a dark patina so that the cracks are emphasized by the dark color.

Waxing

Wax not only feeds and protects wood against staining, it also gives it the sheen and richness of an antique, and adds a fragrance to the wood.

You can add to the aged effect when using wax by marring the finish of the stenciling with steel wool before applying the wax.

1- Apply one or two coats of varnish. When the last coat is completely dry, mar the surface of your stenciling by gently sanding with grade 000 steel wool so that the painted surface looks worn.

2- Apply a generous amount of wax on a soft cloth or grade 0000 steel wool, and extend it evenly over the entire surface. Leave it on for a few minutes and then shine with a soft cloth.

Stenciling on textiles

Textile stenciling opens the door to a wide range of decorating possibilities. Beautiful effects can be added to all kinds of fabric, from upholstery and household linens to clothes, sneakers, and lamp shades. Stenciling can be done fairly quickly, producing colorful and attractive results, taking far less time than embroidery or appliqué, though it may perfectly imitate them. With stenciling you can also imitate cross-stitching, festooning, and even patchwork. Stenciling on fabric will endure even with laundering, if the right paints are used.

The types of fabric that can be stenciled

Although it is possible to stencil on practically any type of fabric, before considering stenciling on fabric, certain things need to be taken into account:
• The most suitable materials for stenciling are those made from natural fibers such as cotton and linen or heavy silks, as they are absorbent and the paint penetrates easily, which means the fabric also won't fade easily.
• In addition, you can use materials with a 50 percent mix of synthetic fiber or polyester, or even some completely synthetic fibers. But since heat must be applied to textile paints with an iron, to fix them to the fibers, and many fabrics that are completely synthetic will be damaged by the heat of the iron, it is best to test your fabric first. Before stenciling, iron the fabric, testing its resistance to heat. Do some trial paint applications, if possible, and wash it several times to ensure that it is colorfast.
• The texture of your fabric will play a role in the look of the stenciled design, but whether the fabric is fine or heavy, stenciling can produce some wonderful results.
• The color of your fabric is also an important factor. If the color is very dark you will need to use paints of light, dense colors for them to be visible. Some manufacturers make paint in opaque colors for use on dark fabrics.

Stenciling onto fabric produces some very exciting and creative work. It also presents the opportunity to coordinate stenciling with elements of sewing, the use of different-colored threads for edging, adding lace trims, buttons, rickrack, ribbons, beads, and anything else you can think of that will add visual interest and texture.

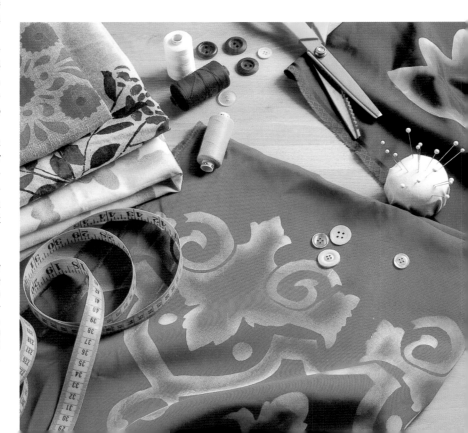

From top left: cross-stitch material, linen, sailcloth, cotton jersey, burlap, curtain chiffon, dark fabric, silk, poplin, cambric.

This stencil done on cotton cambric has shadowing that gives definition to the lion's form.

Silk is a perfect material for stenciling with shadows and volume because its sheen tends to highlight form. Because of the sheen factor, it is best to use simple designs and fewer colors; a busy design may begin to break apart with the reflected light.

This burlap has been stenciled with a large design and the outlines have been emphasized to make the form clear against the prominent texture.

This navy blue material was stenciled with light, opaque colors for sharp contrast. The bright yellow had to be applied in several layers to cover the dark background. The red areas and shading were done last.

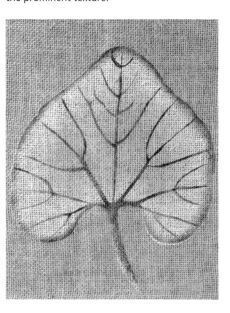

The design on this sailcloth is monochromatic; it is a simple shape but large enough to have a strong impact.

How to stencil on fabric

To begin, organize your work area so that it is clean and free of clutter. This is important, particularly when working with fabrics, as accidents can quickly ruin them. Fabrics are all too easily stained by a dirty brush carelessly placed, or a lid. Often, these stains can never be removed completely, even though the fabric is washed immediately. While it is true they can be worked over with stenciling, it is, of course, best to avoid stains in the first place.

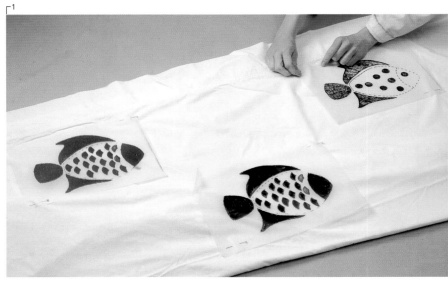

1- Before beginning to stencil, paint the designs first on paper; then pin them to the fabric and check the visual effect and the size of the design. Next, interpret your design into stencils, line up the stencils with masking tape, and draw the marking lines.

2- When stenciling on fabric, the brushes should be slightly damp. Dip them in water and dab off the excess on a dry cloth or paper towel.

3- Mix the base color with white. You will need more paint than usual, as fabric is more absorbent than other supports.

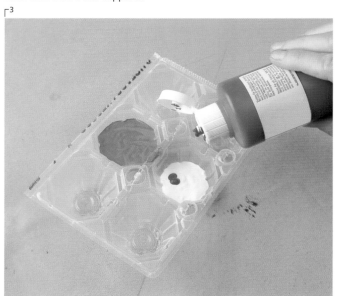

4- Now dip the brush in your mixture and dab off the excess on your paper towel. The brush should be as dry as with previous techniques.

5- Stretch the fabric out on a table covered with kraft paper. This will serve to absorb the paint while protecting the table and fabric from staining. Position the stencil and start to paint, using circular motions, creating a uniform base color in each shape. Use a light touch, trying not to soak the fabric with paint.

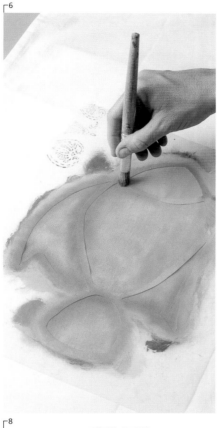

6- Before it is completely dry, paint the shadows with a darker shade of your color. You may want to use the color at full strength, without mixing it with white, for stronger contrast. Use a clean brush and very little paint. If you wish, you can layer colors before they are completely dry. It is simpler to paint and shade all the shapes in the design before lifting off the stencil, rather than struggle to reposition it later. The first layer, the mix of blue and white, penetrates the fabric and acts as a primer to fix the colors layered on top.

7- When the first stage is completely dry, put the second stencil in place.

8- Paint in the darker colors. Here, we've used the blue without mixing it with any white.

9- Here is the finished stencil design as it appears on the pillowcase. The sheets are done the same way.

10- Generally, you should allow the fabric to dry for three or four days. Then iron it with a hot iron and no steam. Iron for two or three minutes on both the painted side and the back to fix the colors. Wait another three or four days before washing.

The importance of the base color

As with any other surface, when stenciling onto fabric you'll do best when the shapes are transparent and carefully modeled with light and shade in the ways we have discussed in previous chapters. To achieve the desired effect, paint the base color at the center of your shapes, which will give them a light focal point. This bright spot will work with the darker shadows at the edges, enriching the work and giving it greater volume.

This base coat will function as a primer, coating the fibers of the fabric so that they become saturated with paint. Then, the work you do using a very dry brush to achieve transparent paint layers will remain fast, rather than disappearing after the first wash. So, to make sure that the color is properly fixed, you can take a number of steps: Paint the shapes first with a white base that saturates the fibers. Then shade in a darker color, or paint the base in a color that matches the colors you are going to shade with. You can also mix a little white with the general color of the design, paint the base with this mixture, then shade with un-diluted dark paint. This will, in one step, create the soft shadows of layered colors so typical of stenciling, while providing the support with the holding power that will prevent your colors from fading despite frequent washing.

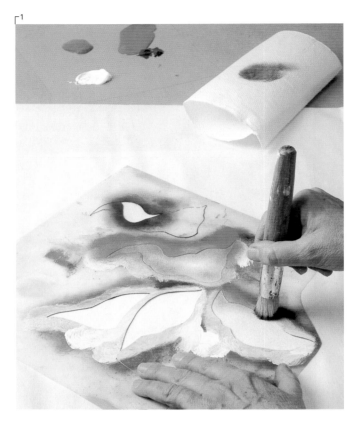

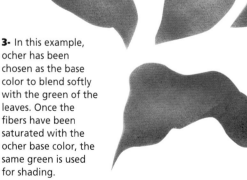

1- In this example, we want to keep the white of the material as a focal point of light in the center of our shapes. To do this, a white opaque base is applied to saturate the fibers. Before the white is completely dry, the leaves are shaded in green.

2- Here are the stenciled leaves, the result of the above process. The center is the same color as the fabric and the leaves are modeled with all the nuances of light and shade.

3- In this example, ocher has been chosen as the base color to blend softly with the green of the leaves. Once the fibers have been saturated with the ocher base color, the same green is used for shading.

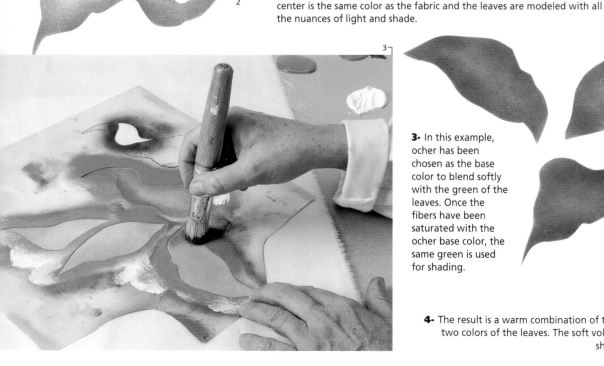

4- The result is a warm combination of the white of the fabric and the two colors of the leaves. The soft volume expressed with the green shadows makes the leaves glow.

Before starting to paint

Wash the fabric to remove any starch and allow it to shrink, especially when using cotton. Let it dry, and iron it to remove creases that could cause blank spaces when stenciled.
If you are stenciling material to upholster with, it won't be necessary to wash it but it will need ironing.

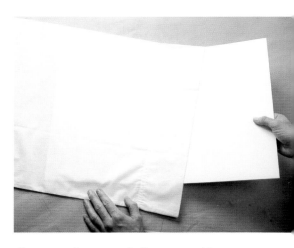

Make sure of the size and measurements of your design; it is harder to compensate for mistakes with fabric as the surface cannot simply be repainted. For this reason, it is a good idea to cut the shapes out in paper first and pin them onto the fabric to check the effect and confirm the size of the design.

If you are going to stencil pillowcases, T-shirts, or other items of clothing, put a piece of heavy paper or cardboard between the fabric to be stenciled and the fabric underneath so that the paint does not soak through.

Mark the correct position of the design with a nonpermanent marker such as tailor's chalk, which you can buy at a notions, craft, or art supply store. It usually comes in light colors. It leaves very clear marks but brushes off or disappears with the first wash.

Use masking tape to line up the stencils on large pieces such as sheets, tablecloths, and curtains. Once the tape is in place, you can draw your stencil shapes or any other essential line in pencil. Keep your lines to a minimum when working with fine fabric such as cambric or organdy, as these fabrics are less likely to be laundered or frequently cleaned. A light pencil marking will do just as well as nonpermanent marker. On the other hand, a marker is ideal for use on heavy fabric such as canvas.

Stenciled household linens

By using stenciling you can match your household linens to the designs on the walls or a dinner service. It is also fun to match a baby's nursery walls and furniture with pajamas, sheets, and favorite articles of clothing.

One can even use stenciling designs as a substitute for embroidery on tablecloths, nightclothes, and sheets with very beautiful results. Pale colors are used to paint light fabric such as cambric, linen, and silks. Embroidery designs can be a wonderful source of inspiration and a guide for the design of your stencil.

The same teddy bear design has been combined with others to decorate these sheets, the towel, and a pillow for a baby's layette.

The motif from a tea set has been used to decorate some breakfast place mats.

The designs stenciled on the walls have been repeated on the bedspread and the curtains in this child's bedroom.

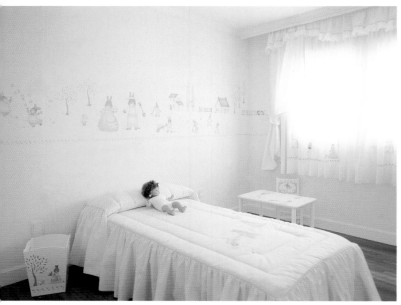

Place mats and napkins are easy to do, especially for beginners.

Imitation cross-stitch

To imitate cross-stitch designs using stencil, cross-stitch books are an excellent reference, where you will find each of the colors of a design represented as a series of crosses in boxes. Here, you can simplify the design and transfer it, drawing its shapes onto the stencils to cut them out.

The ship design from the cross-stitch book has been simplified and the outlines have been drawn in step-like marks to imitate cross-stitching. The color scheme is also simplified to only four colors.

This picture of a tall ship has been stenciled, although it has the look of cross-stitch.

Draw out your stencils with right angle-type step marks around its edges to reproduce the look of cross-stitching. Now stencil the design onto cross-stitching linen. Use flat color without shadows.

Imitation appliqué

Appliqué consists of sewing a shape cut from a piece of fabric onto another fabric of a different color, then tucking and stitching the edges. Imitation appliqué looks lovely when stenciled on fine fabric such as cotton cambric.

Once the designs have been painted and shaded on the fabric, you can outline them freehand in a very dark color, or you can stipple the edges with a very small stenciling brush and the darkest color in your design.

Imitation embroidery

This technique is very effective for painting initials or other designs that are characteristic of embroidery on sheets, pillows, and other linens. Since festooning is generally raised, this too must be reproduced with stenciling. To achieve a raised look, shade around the edges, adding some gray to the color you are using.

The shadows should be extremely subtle so that the stenciling conveys the delicacy of embroidery; they should therefore be done before the base color has dried completely so that they can be blended. If the shapes are very small, another way to give them a raised look is to go over the edges freehand with a very fine brush.

This stenciling motif was inspired by an antique organdy tablecloth, embroidered and appliquéd.

Paint both the initial and the shape of the festooning in a light color such as white, pale blue, pink, or yellow. In this example, a white cambric cushion has been painted with beige.

Stenciling patchwork

Patchwork quilting was one of the most widespread popular craft traditions in North America during the first 60 years of the nineteenth century, and it continues to be today. It is used to make bedspreads, quilts, and cushion covers, by combining many pieces of different-colored or patterned fabrics. When sewn together by hand, these small pieces form larger patterns. The whole piece is then stitched to fiber batting, which gives it body and volume. Further patterning is then stitched or quilted into the surface, in the same color or contrasting thread, to hold the batting to its patchwork top.

Stenciling is simpler and takes less time compared to the effort involved in cutting and hand sewing a quilt piece by piece, and it has a lovely look of its own. The best fabrics for stenciling patchwork are cottons, linens, and even fine burlap, which will give your piece a rustic air.

There are many popular traditional American designs. They are very simple, almost primitive, patterns consisting of hearts, clovers, flowers and leaves, and other plain motifs. It is best to use large, simple shapes when stenciling imitation patchwork, rather than shapes that are small and intricate. There are books devoted exclusively to patchwork techniques, and they are wonderful sources of inspiration for stencil design.

This photo shows a hand-sewn patchwork that is made with many fabrics.

Hand-stenciled patchwork. The volume of the stenciled shapes is defined and reinforced by the batting and machine stitching around the edges.

To make this small stenciled quilt, you will need fabric paints and all your other stenciling materials, two pieces of cotton 36 × 36 inches (one to stencil, the other for the backing), cotton batting 36 × 36 inches, a tape measure, thread the same color as the fabric, a needle, scissors, pins, tailor's chalk, and sticky tape. This quilt can be sewn by hand or machine.

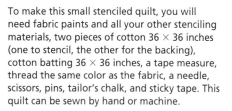

1- Wash and iron the material. Spread it out fully so that it lies completely flat on the floor or a large table, and then anchor it.

2- Leave a margin of 1 inch around the edges for hems. Mark the margin with tailor's chalk. Divide the central area, which should measure 34 inches, into four equal parts, marking a cross with tailor's chalk. Divide each of these four boxes into four equal parts, using the same procedure, to have squares of 8½ × 8½ inches.

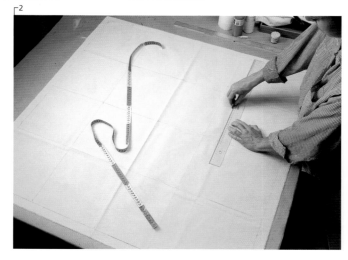

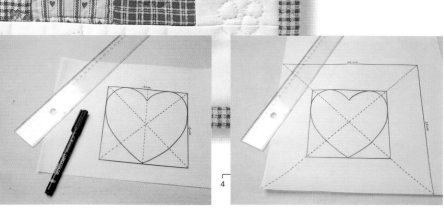

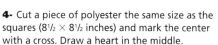

3- Adapt the pattern shapes to fit the squares and then make the stencil. Draw a square 5 × 5 inches and draw a heart in the center. Mark the center of the heart with a cross.

4- Cut a piece of polyester the same size as the squares (8½ × 8½ inches) and mark the center with a cross. Draw a heart in the middle.

5- Cut out the heart with a craft knife.

6- Place the stencil on the material so that it lines up with the edges of the square.

7- Paint the heart in different colors, alternating them, following the instructions given in How to stencil on fabric (pages 102–105). Shade the edges to give the shapes volume.

8- Paint the horizontal and vertical lines that mark the squares in navy blue, using a stencil in which you have cut a space 8½ × 1 inches.

9- Leave the piece to dry for a few days and then iron both sides with a hot iron without steam.

10- Finally, sandwich the batting between the two pieces of fabric. Machine-stitch around the edges of the hearts and hem the edges of the quilt.

Stenciling
on upholstery

In the same way as furniture can be re-
finished using stenciling, you can also
transform curtains and shades, sofas, and
chairs, the material of which is a little
worn but still too good to throw away.
It's fun, and above all inexpensive, to
buy plain, hard-wearing cottons and stencil them to cover or patch an armchair
or a footstool. It is a way to add original decorative touches to a bedroom, living room, or study. Even simple fabric
such as canvas can be transformed into a
work of art to coordinate with the walls
or furniture. If the furniture is already
upholstered, it won't be necessary to fix
the colors by ironing, although if you
use dry-cleaning products on them, test
them first for colorfastness.

Stenciling is
particularly
recommended to
decorate shades. Be
careful to space your
motifs so that they
are clearly visible and
don't fall on areas
that fold when the
shade is raised or
lowered. The motifs
stand out against the
light, so it is
important to be very
precise when cutting
out shapes and when
layering colors and
shading.

This stool is in a decorator's studio. When the
old plastic covering ripped, it was
reupholstered in cotton fabric stenciled with
an enormous red flower.

These stenciled, removable back covers add a
touch of elegance to these dining room chairs.

This nursery chair has been given an attractive personal touch stenciled with the baby's initial. You don't have to remove the material to stencil furniture.

The headboard of this bed was covered in tan sailcloth and stenciled in white, using stencils designed with the look of the little girl's drawings and handwriting.

Stenciling a footstool

To stencil something that is already upholstered, like this footstool, it is not necessary to remove the material; you need only stencil directly onto it. As it won't be washed in a washing machine, you will not have to saturate the fibers of its fabric, so, if the background is an interesting color or would be useful for creating light and shade, it is not essential to apply another light opaque base color to create shadows unless the design calls for it.

1- If the legs can be easily removed, it is better to take them off to work more comfortably with the top section resting on a worktable. For this burlap covering, we have chosen a Native American theme for the design. It needs no light base color applied to it, as the color of the fabric works perfectly with the colors chosen. The first motifs are stenciled in a rusty red.

2- The central motifs are stenciled in blue, bright yellow, and black, allowing the beige of the fabric to show through in the middle.

3- Here is the footstool once the stenciling is complete and the legs are put back on. To protect it, iron it to fix the colors. Don't use steam as this will dissolve or damage your colors.

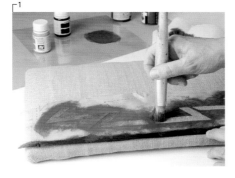

Stenciling on other surfaces

Once you have discovered the endless possibilities stenciling offers for decorating any object or surface, you'll find it such fun and be so pleased with the results that you will soon want to use it in a host of ways, from the most obvious, such as rugs and mats, to lamp shades, to more unusual things, such as umbrellas, writing paper, and even cakes.

This lovely set of stenciled designs matches napkins, eggs, cards, and napkin rings, all with the same pattern.

This kitchen cupboard has been decorated by stenciling the glass door, imitating glass etching.

Stenciling onto lamp shades

Stenciled fabric or paper lamp shades have a special charm as each color is highlighted by the light that shines through from underneath. Stenciling not only enhances new shades but can hide stains on an old one. In any case, it is important that the edges of your shapes are well-defined because, as with a window shade, any flaws will become obvious because of the light that shines through its surface.

This fruit design is rather complex. Since it can be difficult to fix the stencil firmly over the curve of the shade, work up to more complicated patterns slowly.

If you want to use new material for your shade but keep the old frame, you can take the shade apart, spread out the old shade, and use it as a template to make your stencil, using polyester or manila paper. This will make it easier to lay out a geometrical border or a central motif. Working flat is best for any design that requires careful measurement or uses equidistant shapes if you want to decorate several lamps with the same design. It is much easier to stencil the shade before you mount it on the frame.

If the shade has already been mounted, work your design in small sections. Simple friezes are easier to manage in this context, compensating for the curvature as you work. Another good possibility is to use a simple design and to paint freely without concerning yourself with precise spacing.

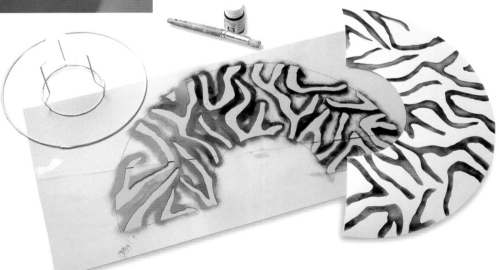

Stenciling on vegetable fibers and cotton

Natural vegetable fibers, such as sisal, coconut, and cotton, which are used to make rugs, carpets, and upholstered panels, make excellent supports for stenciling. In fact, many items made from natural fibers, such as straw hats, raffia bags, and doormats woven of various grasses, can be brought to life with stenciling. When stenciling a contoured object, the stencil will never lie completely flat on its surface, so take special care when you paint. See that your brush is kept dry so that the paint won't run beyond the edges of your stencil. Fabric paints can be used on carpets, as they keep their color well despite heavy use. You can also use acrylic paints if you varnish the surface once the work is completely dry. Then, simply replace your stencil carefully over your shapes and use acrylic varnish with a stencil brush.

Sisal and coconut mats come in various weaves that will affect the choice of design. Use large, simple designs on the coarse, rustic weave of coconut matting, as small shapes and subtle shading will get lost.

To paint a simple woven grass welcome mat, use a stencil brush and small brushstrokes. Choose large designs, such as this rooster, and work without shading, as the material will not accept such subtleties.

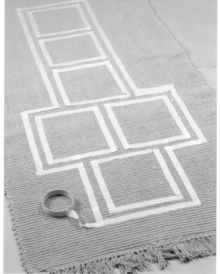

It is difficult to get the stencil to lie without gaps on a coarsely woven mat. In this example, since the design was geometrical and linear, we simply used masking tape.

Once we had painted the outlines and removed the masking tape, we stenciled in the hopscotch numbers. It is best to use a simple design on a coarse weave cotton mat such as this one.

On fiber mats that have a finer weave, you can stencil with soft shading and use designs of varying sizes.

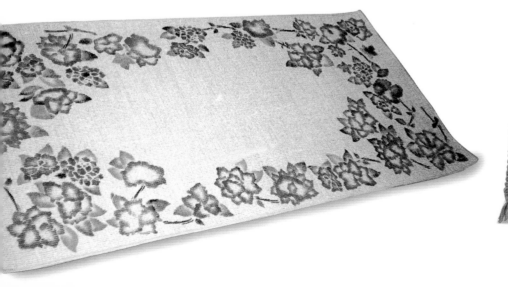

Stenciling on paper

Paper is probably the easiest support to stencil on. Paper stenciling is popular for children's projects as well, as many different media can be used, such as colored pencils, marker pens, and crayons. You can use this method to personalize an endless number of objects, such as writing paper, envelopes, and birthday cards. Stenciling can be used to decorate paper for wrapping presents and to cover storage boxes. It will make party things of ordinary paper tablecloths and napkins.

Instead of buying gift-wrapping paper to wrap your presents, it can be more original to stencil on plain paper or boxes. If the object to be wrapped is soft, you can decorate the paper before wrapping. If it has a flat, hard surface, it can be painted after wrapping.

Some tips on stenciling on paper

• Stencil brushes should always be very soft and, above all, as dry as possible when painting.
• In general, use very absorbent paper. If your paper has a glossy finish, you can stencil by tapping gently.
• You can use any type of paint you choose. Acrylic is practical, as it dries quickly. Oil paints bleed on an absorbent paper surface and produce very pretty effects, both opaque and transparent.
• If the paper is very fine, use paint in stick or cream form, as acrylic paint is too heavy and wet.
• Anchor the stencil with spray adhesive rather than tape so the surface isn't marred or torn when you try to remove it.

Stenciled stationery

A good way to produce a quantity of similarly stenciled paper is to make a right-angled guide with tape and cardboard or illustration board cut the same size as the two dimensions of the paper. Cover your work surface with a sheet of paper. Anchor your guide to the work surface. Now lay down the paper to be stenciled and place the stencil on top. Anchor these to the worktable as well. Using this method, you can quickly stencil envelopes or cards. This is a good way, for example, to make invitations for a special occasion.

1- Using a guide and a stencil makes the production of personalized writing paper no hardship at all, as it can be done very quickly.

2- Cut out a piece of cardboard in an L shape and anchor it to the table you have previously covered in paper. Place the stencil on the guide and anchor it. Be sure the stencil is properly aligned so that the design appears in exactly the right place.

3- Place a pile of writing paper under the stencil and paint using an oil stick as your medium. Oil sticks and stencils create light, subtle results on paper.

4- Once you have stenciled the first sheet, lift the stencil slightly and slide it out. Stencil the second sheet and repeat the procedure until you have stenciled all the sheets of paper.

Stenciling on ceramics

Enameled ceramic objects or glazed tiles are somewhat difficult to stencil on because their surfaces are not porous. This makes for a slippery finish and causes the paint to remain on the surface. Even if you use special paints for cold ceramics—ceramics that have already been fired and glazed—the stenciling is unlikely to stand up to everyday use such as washing with detergents and hot water. It is best not to stencil objects that are constantly exposed to moisture, such as showers or bathroom floors, or that are washed daily, such as crockery or tableware. Stenciling can, however, be used successfully on ceramic objects that are used for decorative purposes.

Cold ceramic stenciling

The technique used to stencil ceramics differs slightly from traditional stenciling. The secret of getting the stencil to adhere firmly to the glazed surface lies in completely eliminating all traces of grease and creating a thick, opaque base color. Special ceramic paints adhere well using this method. If you do not have any, you can use a mixture of enamel, polyurethane lacquer, and polyurethane varnish. In both cases, the procedure is the same. In the following example, we will do some stenciling onto some plates that are to be used for purely decorative purposes.

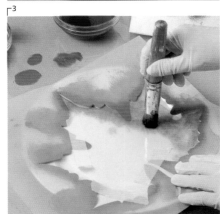

4- When the base has dried completely, you can add the details. With a fine, round brush, paint in the veins of the leaves freehand, using the same color.

1- It is essential to prepare the surface well. Use hot water and a detergent capable of removing all traces of grease until your surface is squeaky clean.

2- Once dry, clean again with nitric acid, allowing it to work for several minutes. Wear a mask and gloves to do this as nitric acid is highly toxic. Besides being a powerful cleansing agent, nitric acid serves to mar the glazed surface, making it slightly porous. Rinse thoroughly and allow to dry.

3- Stick the stencil to the surface with an adhesive spray or sticky tape. It's more practical to use tape on plates as the raised contours make it difficult to stick the stencil down flat. Dip the brush in the mixture of enamel, polyurethane lacquer, and polyurethane varnish, and unload the surplus paint on absorbent paper. Stencil using a stippling technique. Allow to dry completely, leaving the stencil in place, and repeat the process until you have obtained a base of opaque color. As you are using large amounts of paint, be careful that it doesn't run underneath the edges of the stencil. If this does happen, you can remove it by scraping or scrubbing with a scouring pad and detergent before the paint dries.

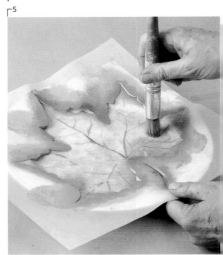

5- When the surface is completely dry and the paint has hardened (after 12 to 24 hours), replace the stencil and apply a coat of polyurethane varnish or yacht varnish by stippling. This will seal the stencil.

Stenciling on terra-cotta

Terra-cotta, or any unglazed pottery, has a highly porous surface, which means it will take ceramic paint well and facilitate creating effects of shadows and transparencies. The surface needs no special preparation, although it should be carefully cleaned and free of grease and dust.

Stenciling on unglazed terra-cotta is easy, as cold ceramic paints adhere well to its porous surface. This enables you to create very subtle effects of shading and transparency.

When stenciling curved objects, you must hold the stencil down with your hands, as it is difficult to keep it completely anchored evenly against the surface. Use circular brushstrokes when painting.

Warm ceramic stenciling

There are paints on the market that require baking in the oven to fix the stenciling onto glazed ceramics. These paints can also be applied to porcelain, pottery, and other supports such as glass and metal. It is best to clean the surface with turpentine before stenciling. Ask your crafts dealer about drying times and temperatures, as these vary greatly from product to product.

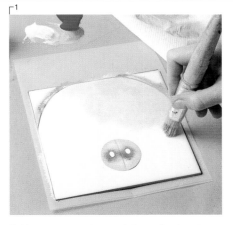

1- Here, we are using a mixture of red and white ceramic paint. The first design is painted onto the tile by stippling, using very little paint. Allow to dry for five minutes.

2- If you wish, give it a second coat to achieve a more opaque color. Paint the second stencil in a darker shade.

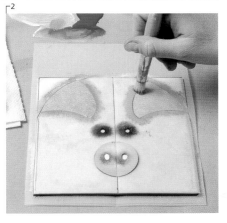

3- Stencil the eyes and nose in brown and allow to completely dry.

4- Fire in the oven at 285 to 300°F (140 to 150°C) for 30 minutes. Once it has been fired, it can be washed, even in a dishwasher.

Stenciling on glass

For stenciling on glass, glass paints offer endless possibilities. You can create the effect of etching on windows, doors, and mirrors, and personalize dishes. Using glass paints on transparent glass allows you to play with light. The leaded or etched windows of old houses not only let in the light, but soften it and maintain the privacy of their occupants.

Glass can be painted with special paint (see page 25), which, because of its ability to adhere, ensures that the stencil will last a long time. However, you can also use automobile spray paint, although it is more opaque.

Once your paint is completely dry, allow some time for it to set before cleaning the glass. Use soap and water and avoid scouring agents and abrasive detergents. Wineglasses should be washed by hand in warm, soapy water.

Advice

The best way to stencil on glass is to stipple and use small stencils if working on curved surfaces. Large stencils are difficult to lay flush.

A milk pitcher and breakfast glasses stenciled with special glass paint. Transform inexpensive, simple glass objects into something charming and original.

Wineglasses can be stenciled with initials that look etched. Imitation etching can be used to decorate windows, glass shower doors, or bathroom mirrors, reproducing antique designs or picking up on tile or towel motifs.

Imitation etching

For this stencil we copied an Art Nouveau wall design. The result is reminiscent of traditional etched windows. Modern designs can also be pretty, translated into stenciled faux etching.

Although most glass paints are transparent, we have used an opaque oil paint for this design, which needs turpentine to remove any mistakes.

2- Use only a small amount of paint on your brush; then dab off the excess on a piece of paper towel. Stipple on the paint using a fairly stiff brush. Start at one end and work your way to the other, taking care to leave no blank spaces. The stenciled shapes should be translucent but covered by an even layer of paint.

1- Remove all grease from your glass surface and mix black and white paint until you have a dark gray. If you are going to paint a window, the gray needs to be fairly dark so that when seen against the light, it reproduces the color produced by the acid in etching (see photograph).

3- The finished stencil: imitation etching.

Colored stenciling

One of the best things about stenciling is its ability to transform a simple object into something attractive and original. In this exercise, a few simple and ordinary glass bowls have gone from being simply practical to becoming table decorations, adding an attractive touch of spring. They could be filled with water and small, colored, floating candles. Stenciling on glass should be done only on the outside, especially on objects used for eating.

A simple daisy design stenciled in various colors has transformed these bowls into dishes suitable for even the best-dressed table.

1- Once the glass has been thoroughly cleaned, turn the bowl upside down and place the stencil on the outside of the base of the bowl. Don't use spray adhesive as it will stain the glass. Hold the stencil with your free hand or use tape to anchor it. Stipple on the first coat of paint. This first coat should be very transparent. To achieve a more opaque color, let the paint dry a bit without removing the stencil, then apply a second coat.

2- To work in the shadows, begin by stenciling with the lighter colors first. In this example, we have stenciled the center of the flower yellow. When it is dry, stencil over the yellow in a darker color. Here we've used red. When the bowl is turned right side up, the first coat of yellow is visible.

Stenciling on metal objects

Practically any metal surface can be stenciled. It is quite common to stencil zinc objects; however, if we take a look around us, we'll notice many more metal objects than we would think: household appliances, iron ceiling beams, often left visible in modern architecture, bicycle helmets, cars, motorbikes, and so on.

Just as with walls and wood, before starting to stencil on metal, you must prepare the surface properly.

Preparing the surface

Household appliances, or any other enameled metal object in good condition, will need only to be cleaned.

If the paint is in bad condition, it is best to repaint it. Sand the surface to make it porous and apply a coat of sealant and a coat of matte or satin-finish gloss paint, using a sponge roller.

If the object has not been painted, clean it and paint it with sealant for metals or nonstick surfaces. When it is completely dry, apply two or three coats of satin-finish gloss paint. In some cases, you can stencil directly onto the object just as you can with zinc.

This exquisitely stenciled iron tankard had practically rusted away. Stenciling restored its lost dignity.

This old metal chocolate box was about to be thrown away. Instead, it was painted black and decorated with the images of chess pieces. Now it makes the perfect gift for a lover of the game of chess.

Stenciling on zinc

Although zinc is a relatively cheap and simple material, stenciling it makes it particularly attractive. As it is not very porous, it is important to remember to apply a coat of sealant before painting so that the paint will adhere properly. For stenciling on zinc surfaces, mix oil paint (from a tube) with matte, satin-finish, or glossy varnish, depending on the effect you want to achieve. In this example, we have used one part oil paint to one-half part varnish.

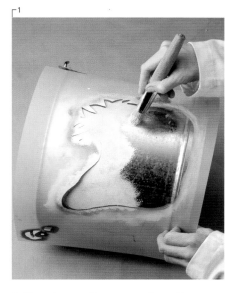

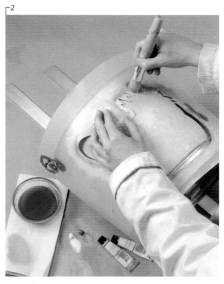

1- Place the stencil on your surface. When stenciling a curved object such as the one shown, hold the stencil in place with your hand as you work in order to keep the edges flat. Apply a coat of sealant, making sure it doesn't bleed underneath the stencil.

2- When the sealant is completely dry, you can begin stenciling; stipple with pale ocher oil paint mixed with a little clear matte varnish. Remember to hold the stencil in place as in the previous step.

Stenciling on brass

Both brass and English silver are nonporous materials, even if they have a matte finish, like this tray. Sealants for metals and other nonporous surfaces will provide the base we need to stencil this type of object. Stenciling on brass or English silver can produce unique and original results.

1- For the design on this tray, we cut out a round stencil. It is then anchored with spray adhesive. Now we apply the sealant by stippling with a thick stenciling brush, applying a second coat once the first one is dry to ensure that the paint will adhere properly.

2- When the sealant is completely dry, stencil with a mixture of red oil paint and a little transparent matte varnish. Stipple on the bright red, making sure it is opaque. To do that, take a fair amount of paint on your brush and dab the excess off on a piece of paper towel. Before the first coat of paint is completely dry, shade with dark yellow in the center of your shapes so that the two colors will blend, creating graded shadows.

3- Remove the stencil and allow the piece to dry for a half hour. Place the second stencil over the tray and stencil the green base of the tomato's stem, using a mixture of green oil paint, a little black, and some varnish. Allow the piece to dry completely before using.

Advanced techniques

Having reached this point, if you have successfully completed several stenciling projects on different surfaces, then it is quite likely that you are eager to know how to carry out more advanced stenciling. This chapter discusses ways in which stenciling can become the perfect tool for creating images that look as though they have been painted freehand, closely depicting reality. The technique known as bridgeless or theorem stenciling is the technique of choice. Even someone who is not really an artist can use this technique to create the effect of *trompe l'oeil. Trompe l'oeil,* a French term that literally means "fool the eye," seeks to simulate reality. It creates the illusion of space where there is no space, and can introduce a note of humor into a design. Trompe combines stenciling with freehand work, perspective, and the representation of light and shade to create volume and the illusion of reality.

Bridgeless stenciling

Bridgeless stenciling, also known as theorem stenciling, is a technique with which it becomes possible to paint an image or motif that creates the illusion of reality. It has been called an art that combines two techniques: designing and cutting out stencils to represent the design as faithfully as possible, and painting it using gradation and transparency to represent volume and shadow.

Origin

There is some evidence that this technique originated in China or India in about the sixteenth century, and for this reason it is sometimes referred to as Oriental Tinting or Poonah Painting.

Bridgeless stenciling was very popular in America in the nineteenth century, particularly in New York State and New England. At that time, it was the practice to educate young women of the middle class in music, painting, embroidery, and many of the decorative arts. Bridgeless stenciling and stenciling in general fell into this category. The principal attraction of bridgeless stenciling lies in the fact that it can be used to create refined floral and fruit compositions that are incredibly lifelike. Motifs that come straight from nature are those that best lend themselves to this technique because its subtle and transparent shading so well depicts them. Theorem or bridgeless stenciling was frequently used to decorate velvet, silk, and linen, as well as being used to paint pictures on watercolor paper.

This bouquet of pansies has been painted using theorem stenciling.

Characteristics of bridgeless stenciling

As its name suggests, bridgeless stenciling consists of depicting reality through the use of an intricate system of stencils. These stencils do not need the bridges or blank spaces that characterize traditional stenciling and that serve the purpose of stabilizing the design and structure of the stencil. Whereas in traditional stenciling you usually use one stencil per color, in bridgeless stenciling each stencil can be used for several colors, as the criterion for differentiating stencils is not color. Once the stenciling is complete, realism can be added freehand, using a paintbrush. A fine outline brush is used, for instance, for flower centers, the veins of leaves, the nuance of shadow, the highlight along a stalk, and so on. The placement of highlights and dark spots requires thought and planning. For instance, it is important to determine the location of the light source in order to represent volume and shadows, including those cast by one shape over another, and to decide on the intensity of the colors, all to convey the look of reality. This requires the delicate control of gradations of colors, as we have been practicing it up to this point.

Sources of inspiration

Just as with traditional stenciling, the sources available for inspiration for theorem stenciling are countless.

At first you may find it practical to consult botanical books and illustrations, or to reproduce the patterns of material, upholstered fabrics, or chintz, which you can find in fabric sample books. The outlines and colors of these are well defined, but when you have some experience, you can look for inspiration in art books, postcard reproductions that can be found in museums, photos, magazines, and nature. But starting simple will help you gather the experience you will need for more complex projects.

You can find inspiration for theorem stenciling in books or swatches of fabric.

How to do theorem stenciling

Both the treatment of the design and the stencil design system for theorem stenciling are considerably more complex and very different from those we have looked at in earlier chapters. The word *theorem* itself has a scientific implication, which is suggestive of the precision required by this technique. A theorem is the expression of a formal system, something scientific, which can be proved. Applying this to stenciling art, it can be said that the sum of all the parts of the design add up, in a rather precise and consistent way, to a complete design that conveys the illusion of reality.

The composition of this design is achieved through the use of a series of stencils, designed and cut out in such a way that intersecting and adjacent areas are not cut from the same stencil. Therefore, before cutting your stencils, the overall piece must be carefully designed to separate the shapes and give them each a number, thus determining the number of stencils necessary to represent the design in its entirety.

Here are some general rules to keep in mind that will help you reduce your design to a minimum number of stencils and make the task of stenciling the necessary areas of light, shade, and volume easier and more coherent:

• Although the stencils are not grouped by color, it is recommended that, before you start, you have a clear idea of which colors you want to use and note the distances between shapes of different colors. In cases where two colors are very close together, it is better not to put them on the same stencil.

• It is essential to analyze the design and take note of those shapes that are on a secondary plane or in the background, or that appear to be behind other shapes, such as leaves that are covered by fruit or overlapping fruit or flowers. Plan the design so that the first stencils you draw and cut out are shapes that appear behind other shapes, and the last cut are those that overlap.

• After you have determined the order of your shapes, check to see whether the darkest shapes are in the foreground. If they are, and if the design allows, place them on the last stencils.

Preparing the design

Careful preparation is essential in order to design the exact number of stencils you will need to construct so that your shapes fit together perfectly.

1- First, locate some visual references for still life or botanical subjects. In our example, we chose a fruit basket and photocopied and enlarged it to the size we needed.

2- Trace the drawing onto tracing paper, outlining the shapes in pencil. Then, divide the picture into numbered shape sections, bearing in mind the proximity of the colors and shapes in the foreground, on a secondary plane, and in the background, as well as determining the location of your darkest colors. Each number will therefore correspond to a stencil; for example, all the sections marked with a number 1 will be drawn on stencil number 1, and so on.

Drawing the stencils

The best paper for theorem stenciling is polyester, as it is transparent and will allow you to see the rest of your design as you work. Cut four pieces of polyester paper the same size, then draw the stencils in the same way as when using the traditional method, although now you won't need to draw a broken line for reference. Number the stencils, from 1 to 4, and draw the shapes you have selected on each of them. The best way to ensure that all the shapes in the picture fit together perfectly is to draw one set of stencils over the others. When each set of stencils is drawn as an overlay of the rest, and when all five sheets are aligned, the design will also be perfectly aligned. Lay the shapes numbered with a 1 over the tracing of the whole design, then lay number 2 down, number 3, then number 4.

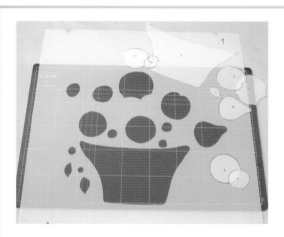

The most practical thing to do is to draw the stencils on top of each other so that the shapes fit together perfectly.

Cutting out the stencils

Cutting out the stencils is a delicate process and though it takes a little patience, you've gathered enough experience now for the task. Precision when cutting is important so that when you are stenciling, the shapes fit together, one perfectly adjacent to the other. For this job, the best tools are the craft knife and scissors. The craft knife especially needs to be very sharp. It is best not to use an electric cutter because it can leave rough edges on the polyester paper and gaps between shapes.

So that the shapes of the various stencils fit together perfectly, a good practice is to cut to the outside of lines drawn with permanent marker pen. All your careful crafting during these stages of preparation is geared to constructing the pieces of your design so that they will fit together without leaving any blank spaces between them, but don't worry if your early efforts do leave a blank space or two. This process, too, requires experience, and gaps are easily remedied. Hold onto your numbered cutouts, as they'll come in handy for correcting mistakes, adjusting shadows, painting veins, and giving leaves volume.

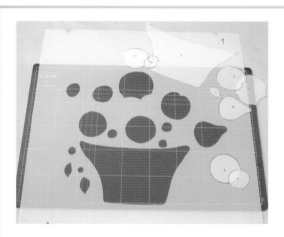

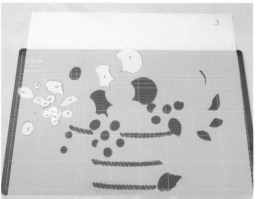

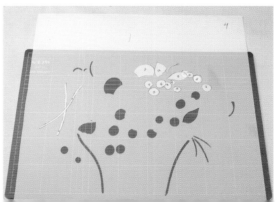

This sequence illustrates the designing and cutting out of the four stencils needed to reproduce the picture of fruit to be stenciled.

Marking the stencils

Along with cutting them out properly, it is very important to mark the stencils so that they line up perfectly, one on top of the other, while you are working. The instructions given previously on making registration marks (shapes drawn in broken lines) are very useful, but because of the numerous layers required for this technique, and because precision is so important, we will add another alignment technique as well. So that each of the shapes that make up the design fits absolutely perfectly, we will use the notch system.

Once you have cut out all your stencils, assemble them so that all the shapes of the design match up perfectly.
To do this, place them on top of the tracing paper original. Anchor them with masking tape to the cutting mat. Cut four triangles, or notches, being sure to cut through all the layers at once so the notches match up.

Preparing the palette

As we have mentioned in previous sections, before starting to stencil it is advisable to have a clear idea of the colors you want to use. For your first experiments with this technique, it is practical to start with a design that is already colored. If the design has many colors, you can simplify it down to just a few in order to reduce your palette. If, on the other hand, the design has no color, then first work out your color system on one or several photocopies of the design before you start working.

Oil paints in stick or cream form can be used with this technique. These lend themselves well to the creation of subtle, transparent shadows. Liquid acrylic paints can also be used, and can be more practical because they dry more quickly. Acrylics will also achieve transparencies and subtle grading of color with a little practice.

Here are the colors we've chosen for our design to be done with theorem stenciling: white, lemon yellow, ocher, pale orange, burnt orange, cadmium red, burgundy, violet, apple green, forest green, red-brown, and dark brown.

Theorem stenciling a basket of fruit

With your paints well distributed on your palette and everything you need set out on your worktable around the surface you are going to stencil, begin the process of painting the design. It is a good idea to work from the original, using it as a guide to choose your colors.

Be aware as you work of the different planes of the design and the direction of your light source, which will cast shadows and darken your background colors while making your foreground colors brighter as they receive more light.

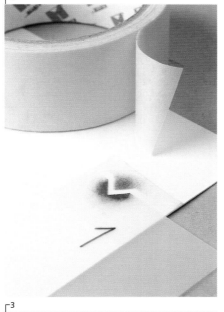

3 and 4- Replace the stencil in its original position and paint the bottoms of the fruit shapes in your base color. The fruit should be stippled to cover the brown completely. The rest of the fruit—the apples and plums—should be painted with circular motions, using the paint lightly and transparently.

1- Place a piece of tape under each of the notches you cut from the stencils, and anchor your stencils to the surface to be painted. With a small stenciling brush and brown paint, paint around each notch, marking each piece of tape.

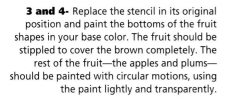

2- Begin by stippling with the first stencil. First, paint the bottom of the basket dark brown. Now lightly block in the fruit in yellow, painting in a pale outline for position. The brown paint should be fairly opaque. Lift the bottom half of the stencil and, using circular movements, very lightly shade the fruit with the brown paint, painting halfway up the fruit forms. This shadow will be just visible through the fruit shapes and will give the impression of depth and density. This is a good trick to use when painting leafy plants and trees.

5- Shade the fruit to simulate volume. The volume of round shapes can be indicated using gradations from light to dark, from the point of light. In our example, the light is centrally located. Shade the edge where the color should be darker. Study the photograph carefully; the color is graded and transparent. Thus you should shadow the edges so that the forms appear round and the edges seem to "lift off " from the surface. Grade the color toward the middle, blending well so that there are no paler areas. This will give the impression of volume. Because the point of light is central, the center of the fruit will appear lighter.

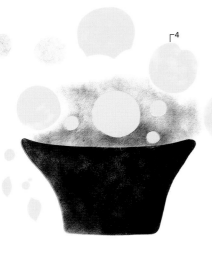

6 and 7- Lift off stencil 1 and place stencil 2 over your picture, making sure the notches coincide with the brown marks you painted earlier on the tape. This will line up the shapes of stencil number 2 with those painted in the previous step. Paint in the bottoms of the fruit shapes first, then the leaves, and shade using circular brushstrokes to create transparent, graded shadows, keeping the point of light in the center. Then paint the weave of the basket by stippling so that the brown you first painted is well covered. Stencil with stencils 3 and 4, following the above steps and paying careful attention to grading and transparency.

Defining planes

If you observe closely, you will notice that shapes that are on top or in front of others cast a darker shadow on the shape below or behind them. In theorem stenciling, these shadows are known as negative shadows. For one shape to come forward, it must be lighter than the shape underneath or behind. This is how we indicate different planes.

To accomplish this, you need the numbered cutouts or cutaway pieces referred to in the step called Cutting out the stencils. To achieve the effect of depth, you can use one of two methods: freehand painting using a very fine outlining brush, and masks.

8- To create depth with masks, first place the cutaway over the shape you want to appear on top or in the foreground. You will know which one to use by matching their numbers. Now hold both in place with your hand, or anchor them with spray adhesive and, using a very small brush and brown paint, shade along the edge that coincides with the shape underneath. This shading should be very subtle and only along the edge.

9- Here is the finished work; the different planes are clear. The shapes on top stand out because of the brown shadow painted on the secondary and background planes.

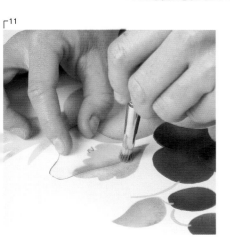

10- Another method of highlighting shapes is to use a very fine brush to emphasize veins and edges. For outlining a fruit shape, use a mixture of its darkest color and solvent—water or turpentine, depending on your medium. For example, if the apple is red, edge it in burgundy mixed with a little brown and solvent. Your mixture should be very transparent so that it blends in subtly with the form rather than standing out on its own. Using a brush, paint the veins of the leaves, stems, and tendrils freehand; add some lines to emphasize the shapes of some of the fruits and touch up any edges that were not cut out cleanly.

11- In the photograph, you can see that we have given the leaves and veins volume using a mask. We used the cutaway shape of the pear because its round shape will work well for drawing graceful veins for the leaf. First, place the curved edge of the pear shape on the center of the leaf. Paint a small area, very sensitively, in the same color as the leaf. Then create the contours of the veins by painting, along the same side of the mask, for each vein, again very sensitively, covering very small areas, always in the same color as the leaf.

12- Once you have shaded the shapes to add depth to the design, adjust the light and shade to give consistency to the whole. This means that the shadows and forms that receive the most light will be lighter than the shapes that are farther in the background and that, therefore, receive less light. For example, the apple on the top right-hand side has been darkened to convey its location on a tertiary plane. The same has been done with the pineapple in the center. This unifies the composition by conveying one consistent light source. A good way to know which shadows need to be darkened and which forms need lightening is to look at the picture through half-closed eyes when you think it's finished. When you blur the details in this way, you can better appreciate the play of light and shade. Once you have adjusted your shadows and lights, add a few hand-painted touches to enrich the whole: white highlights on the apples, the diamond shapes of the pineapple, tendrils and stems, and volume lines for the pears and apples.

Stenciling trompe l'oeil

Trompe l'oeil is a decorative device that enables us to add a little magic to our surroundings. Using trompe, we can open up small places, decorate with marbling or wood finish where none really exists, or create the illusion of landscapes on the flat surfaces of walls and doors. The pleasure and sense of humor intrinsic to this technique lie not in the deception itself, but in the moment the observer discovers the deception.

What trompe l'oeil is

Maurice Denis warned painters with these words: "...Remember that a painting, before it's a war horse, a naked woman or an anecdote, is a flat surface covered by some kind of paint."

Trompe l'oeil is French for "deceives or fools the eye." And trompe does just that—it is a way of fooling the eye by creating the optical illusion of three dimensions that makes the observer doubt the reality he or she is seeing. In short, the purpose of trompe is to induce the eye to accept as real something that is only painted. As Fabrizio Clerici said in the magazine *Plaisir de France:* "The ideal trompe l'oeil is one that represents an object, a landscape, a human figure, or an animal so well that it can even deceive an animal," just as in the legend about the fruit depicted by an anonymous Greek artist, which the birds tried to eat.

The Greeks and the Romans used

Trompe l'oeil is being used more and more to decorate the solid walls of buildings.

trompe l'oeil as one of their most re-fined forms of artistic expression. The Roman artists, Apelleas and Soso de Pérgamo, earned their fame as masters of the art of trompe l'oeil. Trompe developed in various forms in Europe, depending on the taste, cultural background, and nationality of the artist. The great Italian masters of Renaissance painting, such as Giotto, Andrea Mantegna, and Paolo Veronese, used some of the techniques in their frescoes and large murals painted in palaces and churches. In the Low Countries, the influence of trompe l'oeil is felt in paintings of architectural themes and realistic religious paintings, but its scale and support type differ. Dutch and German Renaissance painting was done on boards or canvas in the form of diptychs or easel works. Renaissance themes include everyday objects, musical instruments, cards, and even false curtains. Trompe reached its peak of refinement in the seventeenth and eighteenth centuries when it was even used to make painted panels cut in the form of people and household objects to be used for practical purposes such as screens or fire guards, or to decorate furniture.

In Spain, trompe l'oeil was never considered a real art form. In fact, the French trompe l'oeil was translated in the sixteenth century as "deceit," which may give some indication of its unpopularity with the Spanish culture. However, some Spanish painters did use the technique, among them Murillo, Zurbarán, Carreño de Miranda, Goya, Picasso, and Dalí.

Today, trompe l'oeil is used on a far larger scale than easel painting and is growing quite popular as a medium in the field of the decorative arts. Though trompe is used decoratively, it is again considered a fine art.

Creating the illusion of curtains or drapes is fun, attractive, and adaptable for decorating all kinds of walls.

The most enjoyable thing about these painted shelves is that they aren't shelves at all, but the doors of a small cupboard.

Trompe l'oeil and theorem stenciling

Painting in the tradition of trompe l'oeil requires mastery and expertise and great skill in drawing and perspective. Trompe l'oeil uses perspective to create the illusion of depth and space. Objects painted in trompe seem to lift off the surface they are painted on, so that they appear real. Theorem stenciling is a technique that can be used to depict a motif in a way that is realistic yet simple, with a realistic representation of light, shade, and volume. While trompe l'oeil depicts depth and shadows using all of reality as its themes, theorem stenciling is merely decorative. It is its light, decorative character that makes theorem stenciling ideal for those without the years of training required for trompe l'oeil. Stenciling is user-friendly, fast, and when done from the design to the painted, finished product, slowy but surely, it is quite doable.

Procedure for painting a trompe l'oeil

As with theorem stenciling and all stenciling projects, the creation of a trompe l'oeil image requires following a series of steps so that you make as few mistakes as possible and enjoy the work you are doing. As trompe l'oeil is a complex project, it may seem to be slow. However, it is important to follow all the steps, especially at the beginning, because each of them is necessary in order to move on to the next step. After the steps of preparation, the painting is the easiest and most satisfying part of the process.

Before you look for references for your design, be sure of where you want to locate your painting and how big you want it to be.

Sources of inspiration are many and varied. Any photograph, catalog, or book will give you ideas, but it is important to start with simple designs, avoiding images that are too complex. As you gather experience you will naturally move on to more challenging images, and you will have acquired the skills for the task.

In our example, we have decided to paint a trompe l'oeil that depicts an old kitchen shelf with an array of objects typically found on one. Good sources for an idea such as this one are decorating magazines, advertising leaflets, crockery catalogs, and so on. We

chose several types of cupboards for our models and pieces of crockery that most suited our idea and the size of our available wall; then we photocopied them. The crockery was photocopied at actual size.

The base drawing

Although you can draw directly onto the wall with a pencil, it is better to first draw on kraft paper or some other type of thin paper. There you can make mistakes and changes, and your design can be punched with small holes along its edges to transfer the outline onto the wall. Another advantage to using paper is that it will give you a clear idea of the way the design will look in its space. You can then keep this drawing and use it somewhere else.

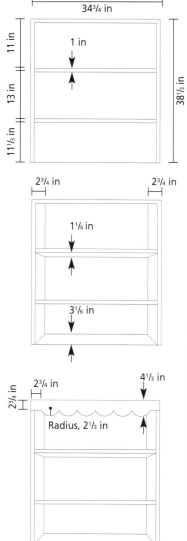

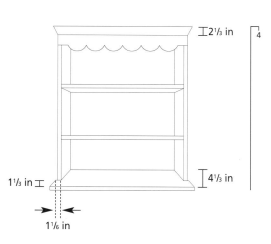

1- On a large piece of kraft paper, draw a rectangle $38^1/_3$ inches tall by $34^3/_4$ inches wide for the central piece of the cupboard, not including the upper cornice or the lower ledge. Draw another rectangle 1 inch inside the first. This represents the thickness of the wood. Draw in the shelves, spacing them by eye, also with a 1-inch thickness.

2- Now draw two vertical lines down the sides, $2^3/_4$ inches from the edge, to depict the depth of the uprights. Then draw the shelves in perspective. Bear in mind that the middle shelf is at eye level, and foreshortened; therefore, only the exterior edge is visible (see drawing). The top shelf is above eye level, so we see it from below. Draw the bottom shelf from above, using the appropriate perspective.

3- Draw the scalloped edge on the top of the unit, using a compass to help you draw uniform curves. Another way to do it would be to trace the edge of something round, such as a glass or the lid of a jar, and extend the ends with straight lines instead of taking the scalloping right to the edges.

4- Now draw the cornice and the bottom ledge. The latter's right and left edges are parallel to the perspective of the bottom shelf. The thickness of all the wood is the same as the shelves.

Composition of the elements

This step is very important and determines the design of each stencil, as you need to determine where you want to place each object on the shelves, and the placement will determine the perspective you must draw each with.

As the lower edge of each object in reality would not be visible sitting on the top shelf, especially if the objects are at the back, and since our idea is to place the plates as though they were leaning against the back of the unit, we have folded the photocopy a little at the bottom.

At eye level, you would see the whole of the objects, face on, with the bottom edge appearing straight. Below eye level, things appear to tip or to lean toward the observer, so you can see some of the topmost plane, and the curve of the lower edges.

Set up the photocopies, factoring in the perspective those objects would take on, depending on their position. In this design there are three viewpoints: a high viewpoint or above eye level (top shelf), eye level (middle shelf), and below eye level (bottom shelf).

Here is a cup shown in three different viewpoints. The cup at the top corresponds to the high viewpoint, the middle cup to eye level, and the bottom cup to the low viewpoint.

How to transfer the design onto the wall

Before transferring the design to your chosen support, remember that the support must be prepared properly. In this project, we are going to stencil with acrylics onto a wall, so the wall must be prepared with matte plastic paint. If you want to stencil a piece of furniture, remember to use the same type of paint. If your surface—wall or door—is painted with gloss or oil-based paint, the trompe l'oeil should be painted with oils.

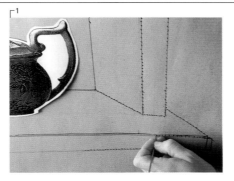

1- Using a fine spike or a bodkin—a tool designed to puncture cloth—perforate the whole design following along the outlines. The holes should be close together and large enough so that later the powdered pigment can go through them. Make sure you perforate all the lines of your drawing.

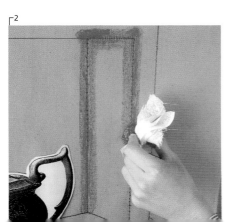

2- Anchor the kraft paper to the wall, positioning it using masking tape. Make a pounce bag—a cloth bag tied at the top—with blue pigment or some other dark color inside (see chapter 2, Paintbrushes and other applicators). Tap over all your perforated lines, making sure the pigment goes through the kraft paper and marks the wall. To be sure that it does, lift the paper up now and then and check.

3- Here you can see what the kraft paper looks like once you've transferred the design onto the wall with the pounce bag. If you want to keep this design for further use, clean off the blue pigment with a dry brush or a cloth. Then roll the kraft paper up and put some masking tape around it for storage. Once you have removed the kraft paper, the design can clearly be seen, printed onto the wall.

Stenciling a trompe l'oeil

First, prepare your palette to have all your colors at hand. To paint this trompe l'oeil piece, we will use acrylics in the following colors: natural umber, burnt umber, white, cobalt blue, pale gray, cadmium yellow, leaf green, yellow ocher, red, and dark red.

Before you begin stenciling, choose a source of light that will illuminate the objects you paint. If there is a light on the ceiling or a window nearby, it will work very well to imitate its light source for the painting of your piece.

Before you stencil your trompe l'oeil design, paint the surface onto which the piece will go. In our example, both the color and the shape of the wooden shelf will determine the colors of the light and the shade.

Next, cut out all the stencils necessary

for each of the objects to be painted on the three shelves. Make sure you have plenty of white paint because you will need it to block in your objects, to hide the wood background. Begin by stenciling the objects on the bottom shelf, then move to the middle shelf, and finally do those on the top shelf.

Colors used in this project.

1- First paint the back, the sides, and the shelves of the unit. Cut two pieces of mylar strips, about 2 inches (6 cm) wide. Hold them with one hand against the back of the image of the shelf and, using your brush dipped in raw umber but very dry, brush up and down, pressing harder in some places to make the strokes more obvious. In other places, paint lightly to vary the shades of the grain. This uneven effect will create the appearance of antique wood planks.

Now move the strips to the next section and repeat. The shelves, the upper ledge, and the cornice are painted using horizontal strokes. Shade the vertical lines at each corner of the uprights to give depth. Do some shading underneath the middle shelf.

As you paint, remove the blue pigment left by the pounce bag with a cloth or clean, dry brush.

2- To paint the scalloped edging, cut out two or three scallops from the edge of your polyester paper. Anchor these to the image of the shelf and paint them, moving them along horizontally, following the instructions for the previous step.

3- This is what the unit looks like once you have stenciled the effect of old wood. The shadows help give the piece a three-dimensional look.

4- Draw and cut out the stencils of all the objects, following the directions given for theorem stenciling. Here we have used elements from a white dinner service that has a blue flowered design. A good way to save time and effort is to cut out the flowers for one of the larger objects and use them to paint the other objects as well. This photo shows the various stencils used for the cups.

5- Proceed with the stenciling of the objects on the bottom shelf. Anchor the stencils onto the surface with spray adhesive. Often, as in this example, the color of the painted base has little to do with the color of the elements, in this case, the dishes stenciled on top. Therefore, before you stencil them, you must fill in their forms with a ground color, covering the background, in this case, the wood grain. Use white to stipple in all the shapes, making sure the white is opaque enough to cover the imitation wood evenly. If necessary, give it another coat.

6- A good trick to speed up the drying process between layers of white is to use a hair dryer so that you can stencil almost immediately.

7- Shade the edges of the cups with pale gray. In the example, the light comes from the center left, so the objects appear slightly darker on the right side.

8- To save work and stencils, the flowered pattern of the dinner service has been cut from the stencil for the teapot. In this photo you can see how the same stencil has been used to paint the flowers on the cups. This system is very useful for any trompe l'oeil design, but is especially suitable when painting ceramics and other patterned objects. In general, any design cut from a stencil can be reused for something other than its original purpose.

9- From the moment you plan a trompe l'oeil, the methods you will need to use to create its realistic image and convincing perspective must be thought through. Up to this point, we have discussed a few of them; there are, of course, others. For instance, placing your objects on the same shelf, but in different positions, will tend to increase depth. In our example, one cup is slightly farther forward than the other. Visually, this increases the impression of depth on the bottom shelf because the forms overlap.

10- The bottom shelf with all the objects stenciled.

11- Stenciling the middle shelf. After stenciling the cup and the pitcher in the same way as the other objects, stencil the cake. This object will take six stencils. Again, the white is stippled in to block out the shape. When the white is dry, stencil the chocolate using circular movements, putting more paint around the edges and letting some white areas show through to create the effect of light and shadow.

12- Stencil the shapes for the icing and filling with ocher, using circular movements, painting more densely around the edges.

13- Now stencil the strawberries and the leaves. On the white base, stencil first with yellow. This will add warmth to the green and will highlight the center of the strawberries. Next, stencil with red, allowing the yellow to show through in the center as light, and finish off the edges with the dark red and brown. Carefully assess the illusion of depth and shadow in the overall design. Darken the strawberries that sit farther away than the edge of the cake. When you have stenciled all the strawberries, paint in the little green seeds with a fine outlining brush.

14- Once you have finished the strawberries, stencil the candle and the glass plate. To build the candle's round form and to model the wax drippings down its sides, shade the candle edges in gray. For the plate, use the same color in various shades.

15- Here is the middle shelf with all its objects.

16- Stenciling the top shelf. The next task is to express the perspective and depth of the top shelf. Painting one plate in front of another, creating overlapping forms, will strengthen the impression of the depth of the shelf. In the photograph (on the next page), the plate farthest to the right was stippled with white first; then the same stencil was moved a little to the left and the second plate was painted. The second plate appears to be farther forward.

17- Instead of using the flower cutout from the teapot stencil for the plates, use one of the designs on the vase stencil. This will give the group on the top shelf unity.

18- Painting the plate. First paint the plate that appears to be behind the other (on the right in the photograph). Do this by covering the plate that appears in front with its mask, or cutout. Then place the stencil over the one that appears behind it and lightly shade the edges. Lift off the stencil and the mask. Then place the stencil over the plate on the left and shade it in the same way. This system of using the mask to cover shapes is useful for painting one shape behind the other, whatever the design.

19- To paint the vase of ivy, first stipple the white base of the vase because it is behind the ivy. When the base is dry, anchor the ivy stencil. A good trick to add highlights to the leaves is to first paint a yellow ocher base that will add a warm light. Thus, instead of stippling in white, we use yellow ocher, until the white base and the brown wood are covered.

20- Once the yellow ocher is completely dry, shade the outline in green, leaving the center of the leaves yellow ocher. Remember, the light is coming from the left.

21- After painting the pattern on the vase, gently shade the edges.

22- With a fine outlining brush, mix green paint with some acrylic medium; then paint the stems of the leaves freehand. Try to keep your hand as loose as possible to give the stalks grace and motion, letting them twist this way and that around each other to simulate the flow of growth. You'll find it useful to look at an actual ivy plant and see how intricately its stem and stalks grow.

23- Once all the elements have been painted, the top shelf looks like this.

24- Just as with theorem stenciling, once all the elements on the shelves have been stenciled, it is time to adjust the light, shade, and depth. As this design is very soft, we've decided to touch up only the shadows of the shelf itself. Using the same stencil as for the wood, the corners of the unit have been darkened slightly on both sides. The final result is a magnificent shelf unit to decorate any kitchen, hall, or dining room.

Glossary

Aluminum scourer

Also called aluminum wool or steel wool; ball of aluminum strands used for wearing down or cleaning surfaces. It comes in different grades: 0, 00, 000, or 0000.

Bridge

Blank space separating the shapes of a design for stenciling; necessary to hold a stencil together when cutting out the whole design on one stencil.

Cold ceramics

Technique for decorating ceramics that does not require any firing to fix the colors; durable, even with successive washing.

Crackled varnish

Varnish that has cracked due to the effects of time, temperature changes, or artificial techniques.

Craft knife

Very sharp steel knife available in different widths and thicknesses, used for very precise cutting of soft materials such as cardboard, paper, plastic, and so on.

Cutting mat

Hard rubber surface for cutting on with a craft knife.

Distemper

Paint for walls made by mixing pigment with sizing or some other glutinous substance and hot water. It is vulnerable and impermanent.

Dry brush technique

Technique that consists of eliminating as much paint from the brush as possible by rubbing it on an absorbent surface before starting to paint.

Drying retardant

Transparent liquid added to acrylic paints to slow down their drying time or to make them more transparent.

Dye

Transparent preparation made from pigment and solvent, used for changing the color of wood without hiding the grain. There are dyes of different colors, and many that simulate the colors of different kinds of wood.

Foam plastic

Chemically produced synthetic material, porous and elastic, used for cleaning and for filling upholstery. There are different thicknesses and grades of firmness. It can be used as a substitute for a paintbrush and is a good material for stenciling.

Guard

Piece of cardboard used when stenciling with an aerosol to protect areas you do not wish to paint or to direct the paint onto a specific area to be painted.

Hot ceramics

Technique for decorating ceramics that requires firing in an oven after painting in order to fix the colors.

Kraft paper

A heavy, brown, wrapping-type paper.

Level

Instrument for checking that a plane is horizontal or for checking the difference in height between two points; it contains liquid and a bubble that moves from side to side.

Manila paper

Thick, absorbent paper.

Marquetry

Decoration obtained by placing thin pieces of different kinds of wood inlaid next to each other, sometimes combined with marble, metals, tortoiseshell, and ivory, and used to cover surfaces, especially in cabinetmaking.

Mask

Piece cut out when making a stencil, used for painting shadows or painting other shapes in negative.

Masking tape

Waterproof adhesive tape of different widths that painters use to mark the spaces to be painted, to paint precise lines, or to protect areas from paint.

Nitric acid

Highly corrosive nitric acid solution.

Notches
Small triangular cuts at the edges of stencils, used particularly for theorem stenciling for the alignment of shapes when using numerous stencils.

Oil paint
Paint with a base of natural oils, such as linseed or poppy oil, or synthetic oils such as enamel paints and polyurethane lacquers. These paints are highly resistant to the weather. They are dissolved with paint thinner or turpentine.

Paint stripper
Highly corrosive liquid used for removing paint or varnish from any surface. It does not damage wood but it does damage plastic.

Paint thinner or white spirit
Also called turpentine substitute, transparent, colorless, with a penetrating smell; used as a solvent for varnishes and oil paint, for removing grease from fabrics, and for preparing synthetic camphor.

Patina
Residue or oxidation that colored objects acquire with the passing of time.

Permanent marker
Marker pen that contains ink that cannot be removed with water.

Perspective
Method of representing three-dimensional objects two-dimensionally.

Pigment
Finely powdered mineral or chemical substance that, mixed with a liquid, forms paint of any kind.

Plumb line
Metal weight hanging on the end of a cord; used for determining that lines are perfectly vertical.

Point of view
Height from which you look at an object or a landscape. To achieve a balanced perspective, the reference point is usually placed at the height of the eyes of an average person who is standing.

Polyester paper
Transparent (acetate) or translucent paper or mylar, made from plastic fibers; water-resistant and damage-proof, it is used for technical drawing and making stencils.

Pounce bag
Small cloth bag filled with pigment and used to apply this pigment through holes punctured in a piece of paper or a stencil.

Primer
Paint with great adhering capacity, used to prime surfaces that are not very porous, such as metal.

Registration marks
System for making sure that the different shapes and colors that make up a stenciling design align correctly when painting. Used to align stencils with the surface to be painted or, as with friezes, to ensure that the design remains parallel and straight. They consist of dotted or broken lines.

Roller
Metal cylinder covered with fleece or synthetic sponge, used for painting surfaces.

Sandpaper
Heavy paper covered with glue and then coated with emery dust or powdered glass, which is used as an abrasive for smoothing and polishing metal, wood, paintwork, and other surfaces. Specific types are available for metal and bare wood, as well as those that can be used wet for polishing varnish.

Sizing
A finishing for materials such as fabric, leather, fibers, and paper. Used for stabilizing surfaces before working on them, or as a final coating.

Spatula
Steel tongue-shaped instrument, flat, flexible, and of different widths. Used to apply filler to walls or furniture.

Stencil
Sheet of metal or paper with designs cut out for painting shapes.

Surgical gloves
Very fine latex gloves used by surgeons. Their main characteristic is that they barely affect the sense of touch, yet protect the hands.

Tailor's chalk
Flat piece of compressed pigment used by tailors to mark clothing. Its pigment is completely eliminated by washing.

Theorem stenciling
Technique of stenciling without bridges and windows in the stencils in order to represent pictures or designs without blank spaces between shapes so that the image is realistic.

Tracing paper
Satin finish, sulfur-treated paper used by artists for tracing; not waterproof.

Varnish
Solution of one or more substances, and of various colors, which leaves a fine, shiny, impermeable film. Varnishes can be oil based: synthetic varnish (for indoors), and polyurethane varnish (for floors and exteriors), or water based, such as acrylic varnish (for furniture).

Water-based paints
Paints made with vinyl or acrylic resins that take a water solvent. These are the plastic, or acrylic, paints. They are excellent for both exterior and interior walls.

Window
An empty shape or cut-out area with a particular shape for the purpose of stenciling.

ACKNOWLEDGMENTS

Our deepest gratitude to Quique and Jaime and to our children for all the time we have stolen from them; to our assistants, María Barangé and Maite Ortega, for their dedication and collaboration, and to Adriana Berón for her confidence and her great help.

STENCILING

Original title of Spanish book:
Estarcido

Text and coordination:
Reyes Pujol-Xicoy
Juana Julià Casals

Exercises created by:
Reyes Pujol-Xicoy
Juana Julià Casals

All inquiries should be addressed to:
Barron's Educational Series, Inc.
250 Wireless Boulevard
Hauppauge, New York 11788
http://www.barronseduc.com

International Standard Book Number
0-7641-1549-9
Library of Congress Catalog Card Number
99-76706

Printed in Spain
9 8 7 6 5 4 3